D1142724

AN INVASION OF PRIVACY

An Invasion of Privacy

TERRY LOVELL

KINGSWAY PUBLICATIONS
EASTBOURNE

Copyright © Terry Lovell 1995

The right of Terry Lovell to be identified as author of this
work has been asserted by him in accordance with the
Copyright, Designs and Patents Act 1988.

First published 1995

All rights reserved.
No part of this publication may be reproduced or
transmitted in any form or by any means, electronic
or mechanical, including photocopy, recording, or any
information storage and retrieval system, without
permission in writing from the publisher.

Unless otherwise indicated, biblical quotations are from the
New International Version © 1973, 1978, 1984 by the
International Bible Society

ISBN 0 86065 827 9

Produced by Bookprint Creative Services
P.O. Box 827, BN21 3YJ, England, for
KINGSWAY PUBLICATIONS LTD
Lottbridge Drive, Eastbourne, E Sussex BN23 6NT.
Printed in Great Britain.

To Sue,
Sam, Sophie, Jessica and Elizabeth,
in the hope that this book will help them understand.
To Gwen, Janice, Alexandra and Toby,
in the hope that they will forgive me.
And to Mum and Dad,
in gratitude for giving me all they had.
Above all, to the glory of God,
in the hope that this book might give encouragement
to those who seek to know him through the Lord
Jesus Christ.

Chapter One

It showed all the signs of being a very long and nauseating night. As we sat in my car, the homosexual queen was recounting in graphic detail what he had witnessed in a gay brothel. And what he witnessed, he said, shocked even him: young kids, in their early teens, high on drink and drugs, taking part in sex orgies in a basement sauna and jacuzzi.

He claimed the youngsters were rent boys—straight kids who, on the run from home, turn to prostitution because they are too broke, too desperate or too unloved to care.

On returning to Glasgow, his home city, he had called our local office to tell all. But, as ever, at a price, plus expenses. My newspaper, *The People*, a Sunday sleaze tabloid then competing with the *News of the World* for the number-one slot, was always on the starting block for this kind of story, and a deal was done.

My role was to go to the place with Tony—not, as they say, his real name—to witness the homosexuals and youngsters at play in the basement. He would do the talking, while I, wired up with a miniature tape recorder, would hover around within recording range,

7

trying my best to look like a punter he had just picked up in a city centre bar.

The thought of what lay ahead turned my stomach. There had been a time when it would have been just another job. Nice expenses and a nice byline. Bring on the next one, please. But now, at forty-two, a father of three, it left me feeling decidedly unhappy.

I had over the years been in some seedy low-life situations, mostly in the company of an assortment of villains, but playing a closet homosexual was a new low. Besides, the way I had been feeling for some months I needed this kind of story like Custer needed Indians.

I had worked on a number of investigations involving homosexuals, from vice boy rackets to the sexual activities of a bottom-spanking MP, and I had discovered they weren't the most reliable of informants.

His kind, the kind who talk to newspapers, are like drunks and drug addicts: chronically unreliable, and will say whatever they think a reporter wants to hear to hype up the value of their information.

When he finished his story, we set off for the brothel, where he said he and his 'affair' had stayed overnight while returning to Glasgow from London. We drove through the centre of Manchester and twenty minutes later, in a suburban street some distance from the brothel, I parked the car.

The three-storey terraced building, doing its best to pose as a hotel, had once, I imagined, been the family home of a wealthy businessman in the days when Manchester enjoyed the wealth of the Lancashire cotton mills, but now it was a city centre overspill area, in a depressing state of terminal decay.

A flickering neon box sign at the top of a short flight of stone steps lit up most of the hotel's name. I followed Tony up the steps, through large, ornate double front doors and into a dimly-lit narrow hall.

There was a balustraded flight of stairs on the left, and, on the right, a small drop-leaf table on which lay a book for the registration of guests. Beyond that, also against the wall, was a well-worn two-seater sofa. There was a threadbare carpet and tired wallpaper which was peeling away from the wall in places. Not a resting place for the faint-hearted.

The sheer romance of it all was shattered a moment or two later by the grand entrance, through a door at the far end of the hall, of a man in his late thirties, casually dressed in a vividly-coloured shell suit. He was the manager, or, more accurately perhaps, the madame. He and the informant welcomed each other with dramatic affection, like Heathcliffe and Catherine out of *Wuthering Heights*.

An effeminate youth, barefooted and holding a can of lager, minced through the same doorway. He was in his late teens, and wore a tee-shirt and shorts. Tony introduced me, explaining how we had met earlier that evening and that we wanted to book in for the night. I managed a weak smile, finding it easy to appear a little uncomfortable, in keeping with my role as a nervous closet homosexual.

It was suggested that we have a drink, and the manager led the way into the kitchen. On the evidence of the state of the cooking range and floor, the chef's speciality was salmonella poisoning. From an upright commercial fridge, the manager produced four cans of lager.

It wasn't in our script, but Tony then suggested to the manager's effeminate friend that he showed me the 'leisure facilities'. I really wasn't keen, but I had little choice. A refusal would have been an unusual reaction.

I followed 'Shirley' out of the kitchen and into the hall. He opened a door beneath the balustraded flight of stairs to reveal bare wooden stairs leading to a large cellar area, lit by a solitary naked red light bulb hanging from a low ceiling.

The air was warm, and smelled of disinfectant and dampness. There was a gentle hum coming from two small hot-air heaters placed against one of the walls. The bare brick walls were painted with white gloss paint, some of which was peeling off in small patches, presumably caused by the damp.

Shirley, with can of lager still in hand, took me to the entrance of several fairly large rooms. There was a jacuzzi in one and a sauna in another. A third was empty, although the entire floor was covered with cushions. Finally, I was shown a room containing a bar and several armchairs.

My guide told about the 'chickens'—young boys— who would be in the jacuzzi later that night, once the pubs and clubs had closed. It hotted up about midnight, he explained. His confirmation of what I could expect to see later that night was, for the purposes of the story, very helpful. The quietness of our surroundings ensured that the miniature tape recorder picked up his every word.

A few minutes later we were back in the kitchen, with the manager and Tony still in enraptured conversation. It was almost a pleasure to be back in their company.

By now I had decided to leave at the earliest opportunity. I had seen and heard all I needed for the kind of story that would satisfy the newsdesk. My brief had been to spend the night there. Once, I would have followed the brief to the death. But not any more. No thanks.

After another can of lager, and promises made to meet later in the basement, Tony and I left the kitchen for a bedroom on the first floor. The decor and furniture was in keeping with the rest of the hotel.

The informant stretched his unlovely body across the bed as I explained that as far as I was concerned his allegations had been confirmed, and that very shortly I would be disappearing through the front door.

Ten minutes later, I was breathing the night air and feeling a little cleaner. But going home to my family after a couple of hours in that cesspit was something I couldn't do straightaway. I had to unload the stench somewhere else. I went for a drink.

The following mid-morning, I collected Tony as arranged, at the spot where we had parked the car the previous evening. It was a genuine pleasure to see him to the rail station for his return journey to Glasgow.

Through information he had supplied, tracing the home address of the owner of the hotel—a twelfth-floor flat of a private tower block in Brixton, South London—was not difficult.

A couple of days later, I was standing at his front door, which was cautiously opened no more than a few inches to reveal the face of a teenage boy. I asked to speak to Mr X, and the face disappeared behind the door. A few seconds later, it was opened widely to let me in.

The youth said nothing as I followed him along a narrow hall to a small living room dominated by two large, high-backed sofas, which faced each other across an ornate imitation marble coffee table.

The furniture was pseudo-antique of the early hideous period. The most notable feature of the room was a pungent smell of cat urine.

I sat on one of the sofas, both of which were layered

with cat's hairs. A moment later, a tall, slim man in his early fifties entered the room to give me the kind of effusive welcome that suggested a reunion of long-lost brothers.

His face was gaunt, cavernous, and his features were sharpened by long hair, heavily grey, which touched his shoulders. He carried a sleek, long-haired cat, and another followed and curled up on the sofa next to him.

While I went through the routine of explaining my reason for calling on him, recounting what I had seen and heard during my guided tour of the hotel basement, he sat regally, legs crossed, running extraordinarily long fingernails through the cat's coat.

In a poor impersonation of Noel Coward, he made a histrionic event of inserting a cigarette into a tortoise-shell cigarette-holder and lighting it with a gold Dunhill lighter, which he snapped shut in a dramatic gesture.

As I went through all the sordid detail, he went through all the feigned and predictable reactions of shock and surprise. Of course, he protested when I had finished, he had had no idea such things had taken place. The manager would be sacked immediately.

We both knew he was lying through his well-capped teeth. We both knew it was all a game. But it didn't matter. I had asked all the right questions and he had given all the right answers. I knew that my presence and the questions I had asked had caused him not the slightest concern.

Everything was wrapped up for a predictably sensational story that would read well in the pages of *The People*—and probably double the gay brothel's business overnight.

I anticipated the story making a page lead. But at the Saturday morning editorial conference, where final decisions were made on which stories would be published that week, it had become an also-ran. Apparently it had been a good week for sensation and scandal.

I was surprised that it had been kicked out. A highly-colourful and graphic account of sexual perversion involving young boys was vintage *People* material. But I was more surprised by my reaction: I couldn't have cared less.

There had been a time when that decision would have hit me hard. I would have taken it personally, as a wounding public criticism. With my ego severely bruised, the weekend would have been a miserable time for the kids and the cat.

I would have had one thought in mind—to get back to the office with the aim of getting my byline into the following week's paper, to make up for my 'failure' and restore my sense of self-esteem.

And the bigger the byline, the greater the ego kick. It was a crude equation that was the central force of my life. It really had been as uncomplicated as that.

But now I experienced none of that angry and painful disappointment. Whether the story was used or not was a matter of total indifference to me. I was simply sickened by the part I had played.

Not for the first time, my reaction reminded me that something was going seriously wrong in my life. There was an inner conflict that was causing considerable confusion and concern. It was as if I was being pulled in different directions, both of them attractive, but, for different reasons, both of them destructive.

More and more I was allowing myself to think about the pointlessness of it all, what I was doing to pay the mortgage, and when a gutter press reporter begins to think that way, he is heading for trouble.

But there seemed to be nothing I could do about it.

Chapter Two

I left school at the age of fifteen qualified to swim 100 yards and play in an inter-schools football league, for which I received, respectively, a certificate and a cheap chrome-plated trophy. My mum had thought I should leave to get a job, and the headmaster Mr Jones agreed, for all the good I was doing at school.

It was a reasonable comment. I was not the stuff of scholars: in between staring out of the classroom windows and not doing my homework, I formed a racehorse betting syndicate funded by dinner money, stealing cakes from the girls' cookery classes when the horses lost, and celebrating with twopenny 'singles'—cigarettes—in a local sweet shop when they won.

The career options open to me were either cabinet-making, because I had once made a fruit bowl and a toast rack in the woodwork class, or working as an assistant in a grocery store where, on Saturdays, I stocked the shelves and delivered groceries and fell in love with Irene Poncini, a schoolgirl assistant who worked on the bacon counter.

It was my chain-smoking Aunt Rene who suggested I should be a reporter. She called almost weekly at our council flat in Paddington, London, to gossip with my mum in a kitchen so small you had to go outside to change your mind.

In between bouts of heavy coughing, an early sign of the lung cancer that was to kill her, she would predict our futures from tea-leaves, and curse 'Jonesy', her bricklayer husband who spent much of his life getting drunk in The Brondesbury Arms.

On this occasion the main item on the agenda was what I was going to do with the rest of my life. From within a cloud of cigarette smoke came my Aunt Rene's voice! 'Why don'tcha be one of them reporters? They d'narf earn good money.'

In the absence of more glamorous options, the proposal was agreed and carried. If I wanted to be a reporter, who dare say I couldn't do it? In blissful, youthful zeal, it didn't occur to me that someone so unqualified was being so wildly ambitious.

Until this time, life had been generously uncomplicated. I had grown up in a world where everybody was broke but nobody was poor. There were no social hang-ups or neuroses about who had what or why, because nobody had very much anyway.

It was a two-street community of family and friends and Brylcreem'd villains; of Sunday best suits, bread and jam for tea, an annual week's holiday in Ramsgate, keys under the mat, and Rin Tin Tin and Muffin the Mule on black-and-white telly.

It was a childhood of playing football in the streets, cricket stumps painted on brick walls, and Tin-Can Tommy games—races with trolley carts built of orange boxes and discarded pram wheels; 5th November bonfires which threatened to burn down entire streets, and learning to box in Johnny Street's backyard.

The hard men, in their sharp suits, played pitch 'n' toss outside the pubs on a Sunday afternoon, and

Barbara Clark, who lived in the block of flats around the corner, was going out with Terry Downes, an up-and-coming boxer known as 'The Flying Dustman', and Bert Fosbrey, who lived in the same block of flats and always dressed flash smart, was viewed in awe from afar because he was reputed to know Jack Spot, a much-feared villain of his day.

Our one-bedroomed flat accommodated a family of five—I had two older sisters—thanks to the wonders of put-u-up beds. We had a cold water tap supply only, and a galvanised bath that hung on a nail on the outside wall. Proper baths were taken in the local council baths once in a blue moon.

Upstairs, in the two-storey terraced Victorian house, lived Mrs Brophy, a gentle and timid Welshwoman, whose Irish militant trade unionist husband, Pat, devoted his energies to Marxism, getting drunk on whisky and kicking the life out of her. When she died early, my mum said it was 'a blessed release for the poor cow.'

Below, living on the ground floor for many years, was a divorced woman of Italian origin, of whom little was seen or heard. Then, in the dead of night, she turned up in my mum and dad's bedroom—silent and naked.

She was standing on my dad's side of the bed. He later said he had told her to sling her hook. The next day she was taken to a mental hospital and not seen again.

It seemed a very normal environment where three families lived without much privacy, and yet their worlds existed, for the most part, harmoniously oblivious of each other. There were no locked doors, and the rows, the smells and the noises belonged to everyone. They were part of all our lives.

It was community life in the raw. A foundational pillar was The Albert, a local pub where the saloon bar counsel of fools and street-sharp sages and assorted rogues was always available for the price of a pint, a few quid or a dodgy favour.

An assortment of the pub regulars would sometimes end up back at our flat on a Saturday night, after the last drinks had been drunk, and where the grown-ups had a great time falling down and being sick. The carpet in the front room, where I slept, would be rolled up to protect it from cigarette burns and beer slops and other drunken mishaps.

A regular top-of-the-bill artiste was Tubby, an accomplished master of the two-fingered school of music. With a matchstick-thin rolled-up cigarette stuck to his bottom lip, he was happy to belt out a dazzling medley of 'Knees up Mother Brown'-type numbers as long as his pint on top of our upright piano was constantly replenished.

My mum, who ironed shirts and scrubbed floors to help meet the bills, was the leading light of many a 'beano' to Southend in coaches loaded down by crates of beer. She would invariably offer her repertoire of old-time songs until she ran out of breath.

My dad's life had been a tough one, founded on a childhood which knew little love and much rejection. He spent his adolescent years, from the age of eleven to eighteen, working for his food and board on a farm in Wales after being caught stealing some sweets from a café. When he returned home, he found that he was no longer welcomed by his father and step-mother. They wanted nothing more to do with him.

When I was about twelve years old, I found him lying on his bed one Sunday afternoon crying. He kept saying that nobody loved him. I put my arm round him and said that we did, but it didn't make any difference.

He began to suffer severe depression—my mum swore it always happened whenever there was a full moon—and he went into a special hospital for treatment, where pads were fitted to his temples for charges of electric current to be blasted into his head. It was supposed to calm him down, but it didn't.

The harsh, loveless times of those early years probably left him incapable of articulating his thoughts and emotions. I can't remember a single gesture of love or affection or encouragement, although when I was about seven or eight, he built me a wooden trolley that was the best in the street.

In working-class parlance, he was above all a grafter with his wages on the kitchen table every Friday night. He spent his life in menial jobs, and walked miles looking for work. I remember he worked as a labourer for North Thames Gas Board, then as a road sweeper, then as an office cleaner for the Post Office, until he retired.

He died working—at the age of eighty-two—on a freezing mid-February morning, delivering newspapers on the council estate where he and Mum lived, and where Mum, now eighty-five, still lives. A neighbour saw him go down—it was a massive heart attack.

As he lay dying, he told the neighbour not to tell my mum. 'Don't tell Lou—she'll only worry,' he explained.

The tragedy was that only in death was he able to express a loving concern that seemed so absent in life. I knew he was proud of what I was to achieve, but he never said so. It wasn't his style.

So with my mum sitting next to me on a No. 6 bus, we headed west down the familiar Edgware Road, along Oxford Street, past Piccadilly Circus to Trafalgar Square and the Strand to arrive in Fleet Street, then the world-renowned centre of the British newspaper industry.

Less than a couple of hours later, we were back on the bus—heading triumphantly home. I had got a job in newspapers. Not as a reporter. Not quite. I was joining the staff of the London bureau of the American news agency, Associated Press—as a copy boy.

The event was marked by a trip to Bon Marche in Harrow Road, bespoke outfitters to the working class. My mum bought me a new shirt and shoes as encouragement, and all on tick.

My job consisted of tearing off sheets of incoming news from telex machines, logging their arrival and taking copies to the desks of different sub-editors. There were several rows of telex machines constantly spewing out news from the world's major capitals.

They occupied a large area of the newsroom, at the centre of which was an island of desks occupied by the sub-editors. Next to each desk there was a telex keyboard operator transmitting news from London.

At the far end of the room were three or four large desks which the London-based correspondents covering Europe would sit around. They seemed to drift in and out of the office at will. They wore smart clothes, smoked fat cigars and one, Eddie Gilmore, wore wide red braces with 'Boston Fire Brigade' printed on them.

Whenever I walked past their desks, I would nod nervously if one happened to look my way. I can't recall any of them responding. They didn't acknowledge copy boys. Nobody above the seniority of the switchboard operator acknowledged copy boys.

But there was one friendly face. It belonged to a Scotsman called Don McNicol. He was a sub-editor, perhaps in his late forties, tall and burly, with a generous smile. He always seemed to wear the same clothes: white shirt, collar unbuttoned, sleeves rolled up past his elbows; stained striped tie, askew; dark grey waistcoat, fully unbuttoned, and matching unpressed trousers; black shoes, unpolished. I think it was a one-piece, zip-up outfit which he stepped out of every night.

While I was dropping copy in his tray on one occasion, he asked me what I was going to do for a real job. I told him I was going to be a reporter. He was kind enough not to laugh. I showed him a short story I had written. It was probably terrible, but his comments, I recall, were encouraging. He went on to suggest that I should first try getting a job as a junior reporter on a local weekly newspaper.

He offered to draft the letter for me. It was an offer I seized eagerly as I didn't know how to put a letter together. A couple of days later, Don handed me the draft. It was a masterpiece. Even I hadn't realised how enthusiastic and willing I was to learn.

With the assistance of a media directory, I sent dozens of copies of Don's letter to weekly papers in towns and cities through the country, and even to Scotland, to places I hadn't heard of, much less pronounce.

Don would also point out hopeful vacancies he'd spotted in a newspaper trade magazine and for which he thought I at least stood an outside chance of an interview. It was Don who drew my attention to a vacancy for a junior reporter at the Chiswick edition office of the *Middlesex Independent*.

A letter was sent, and to my amazement an interview was granted, but I can't recall a single detail of the event. Perhaps the shock of the reply induced temporary amnesia. Evidence that the interview actually took place was provided by the letter I subsequently received offering me the job at a weekly salary of £2 14s 7d.

My mum and dad were ecstatic, as was my chain-smoking, tea-leaf-reading Aunt Rene. And so was Don McNicol, who, on my final day as a copy boy at Associated Press, said enigmatically: 'Remember, many are called, but few are chosen.'

The *Middlesex Independent* was a broadsheet with a gothic masthead and style, dull layout and columns of grey verbiage. It matched the cold and austere atmosphere of the newsroom, a small room at the rear of a converted shop in Chiswick High Road, West London.

The editor was slim, very tall, an immaculate dresser and made of cardboard. He sported a trim moustache, waistcoat, cufflinked shirts and wore ties of military design. He invited no familiarity or friendly words. He was addressed by his initials, D.G. He seemed an unhappy man. Unlike Don McNicol, he was not inclined to help or encourage a young lad who was desperately in need of all the help he could get. Smiling did not come easily to him, and spontaneous laughter even less so, although it did happen once, some months after I had joined the paper.

I had been instructed to pick up a photograph of a local pop group from the home of a freelance photographer. After giving D.G. the photograph, he pointed to a member of the group and asked: 'Is he the percussionist?'

'No,' I replied, 'he's the drummer.' My reply had him guffawing for several minutes, his laughter sycophantically echoed by the younger of my two reporter colleagues, a delicate man in his mid-twenties who spent his days pecking fastidiously at his typewriter, and whose disdainful attitude made it clear that he had little time for a young oik from Paddington.

My older colleague, Percy Gee, spent his days covering the local magistrate's court, which he wrote up in copperplate script on quarter sheets of copy paper. His work done, achieved with the minimum of words, he would shuffle off into the night in his grey gaberdine raincoat and brown trilby hat, grunting goodnight to no one in particular.

My main duty was to make regular visits to the local police, fire and ambulance stations where I would laboriously take down in longhand the details of any minor dramas. That was the easy part.

Writing up three paragraphs on a road accident or chip pan fire caused me to break into a cold sweat. I did not know how to put a sentence together. I didn't know how to structure a story. Syntax was a mystery to me.

My best solution was to scan the back issues of the paper for similar stories and then sweat blood to fit the details from my notebook into a similar style. My wastebin would overflow with aborted efforts.

The agony of these days was followed by the agony of nights trying to learn shorthand and typing at an evening school in Notting Hill, down the road from the gas works in Ladbroke Grove where my dad worked as a labourer. Typing I was able to master, but I never got much beyond the 'Ted paid the debt' exercise in the Pitman textbook.

Some six months after joining the *Middlesex Independent*, I was made redundant. I wasn't sure why. D.G. didn't tell me and I didn't have the courage to ask. All I knew was that I had one month in which to find another job in newspapers if, that is, I was going to stand much chance of getting to Fleet Street.

Dusting off Don McNicol's letter, I had by now acquired sufficient confidence to announce that not only was I keen and willing, but I also had some experience. Such was my desperation to stay in journalism that every night, kneeling by my put-u-up bed in the front room, I prayed to a God I didn't know for a job.

The days passed without so much as an acknowledgement. By the beginning of the fourth week of my month's notice, it looked very much as if my career in newspapers was coming to an ingloriously premature end.

But, with a couple of days to go before saying a final farewell to the pleasure of D.G.'s company, I received a reply from a weekly newspaper in Romford, Essex, on the edge of East London. The editor invited me to contact his secretary to arrange an appointment for an interview.

Boy reporter, aged sixteen, was back in business, but to the God I didn't know I gave no thanks.

Chapter Three

If the *Middlesex Independent* was a frumpy, corset-clad matron never happier than when tucked up in bed with a cup of cocoa, the *Romford Times* was a brassy tart ready to give anyone a good time, dearie, for the price of a headline.

She was a seductive, laid-back lady, who flashed bold headlines and big pictures. She was easy on the eye, and you could tell she'd seen a thing or two. I arrived at her rooms in my best, well-pressed Bon Marche suit, ready for the interview on which my future in newspapers perilously hung.

Trailing the editor's secretary across the newsroom to his office, I felt excited simply being in the same room as reporters hammering away at typewriters, and walking past a small island of desks around which sat the news editor and subs. There was also two sound-proofed telephone cubicles. This was big time stuff.

The editor was a large, portly man, perhaps in his mid-fifties, wearing a tweed suit and a bow-tie. His hair was cut very short, giving added emphasis to a bullet-shaped head. The face was magisterial: stern, fat and heavily jowled, dominated by a large, purple-veined nose surmounted by rimless glasses.

Given my lack of academic qualifications and work experience, it was the shortest of interviews. There was very little I could say by way of self-promotion, other than, yes sir, I was very keen and enthusiastic.

Could I write shorthand? Yes, I lied. Ted, by then, had paid the debt and quit night school. And yes, I could type, I replied more truthfully.

But the big lie, the saddest of lies, came when he asked what my dad did for a living. In days when it seemed to matter, and with enough street cred to realise that the right answer could earn some brownie points, I replied that he was a physicist with North Thames Gas Board, where, of course, he was employed as a labourer.

I'm glad to say he pursued the question no further. He probably knew as much about physicists and their work as I did. I have since felt enormous shame over that lie. In mitigation, I can only offer the defence that it was the panic-borne lie of a desperate youngster who knew no better.

But even then, the whole interview was based on deception. The advertisement invited applicants of eighteen or over. I was still awaiting my seventeenth birthday. Nevertheless, the interview went well.

Some days later, I received a letter offering me a job as junior reporter, and a week later I was moving into bed-and-breakfast accommodation in Victoria Road, next to the railway station, ready to impress the world and beyond.

The newsroom of the *Romford Times*, whose plate-glass frontage overlooked a main street, was part of an open-plan office above a major stationery store. It was as light and spacious as the *Middlesex Indepedent* had been dull and oppressive.

The publishers also owned another successful

weekly newspaper, the *Stratford Express*. Both weeklies, particularly the *Stratford Express*, enjoyed reputations for sharp local journalism. Over the years they had both produced reporters who had graduated with honours to the Fleet Street pack.

Several of the subs worked regular casual shifts on the tabloid dailies where their subbing and layout skills were constantly honed. Naturally, the editorial styles of the *Romford Times* and the *Stratford Express* imitated the wham-bam swagger of their big brothers.

My colleagues were an eclectic crew: the chief reporter, a bearded bear of a man, who wore threadbare jumpers, drove a motorbike and challenged local gypsies to drinking contests; a local council reporter slightly to the left of Stalin who returned to the office one night to urinate over the editor's desk; a talented feature writer who insisted on calling everybody 'old boy' regardless of sex; and a film reviewer who spoke Russian.

In the full bloom of acned youth, and unsure of so much, I did my best to earn their approval, but my appearance found me happiest standing in the shadows, where, covered in skin cream, I would hope to quietly glow unnoticed. For their company and their friendship, I bought beer I couldn't afford in the Golden Lion or King's Head on a Friday night, which quickly made me drunk, but all to no great avail.

Through the guidance of the news editor, I gradually learned how to manipulate people and situations; who to speak to and why, what questions to ask and how to phrase them, and how, most important of all, to put it all together for a tight, dramatic story, with a clichéd intro—the vital first paragraph—of no more than twenty words, if not less, followed by one-sentence paragraphs.

An incident was always described in the intro as

either 'shocking', 'amazing', or 'incredible' to create a sense of drama the facts carelessly denied. Quotes were also kept short and sharp to heighten the drama. Never mind the accuracy, madam, feel the passion.

I also learned the good hack's guide to tabloidese, which meant that armed men who rob banks were 'gunshot gangs', ambulances made 'mercy dashes' and fire engines always 'raced to the blaze'; protesting residents—rarely more than two—were always 'up in arms' at local councils who 'drop bombshells'; brat kids who put the family cat in the washing machine were always 'tiny terrors', although sometimes 'angel-faced' if they photographed cute.

Every blonde was 'big-busted', particularly if she was at the centre of 'a storm in a D-cup'; an employer was a 'boss', an employee a 'worker', a scientist a 'boffin' or 'egghead', a senior police officer a 'top cop', and a nurse in a rescue drama a 'golden-hearted heroine' or 'an angel of mercy'.

A man involved in a 'love triangle' or a 'runaway romance' was invariably a 'randy Romeo', regardless of the truth of his sexual prowess, while the other woman, at the very least, was described as 'attractive', regardless of how unattractive she might actually be, while the 'ditched' wife was always 'heartbroken'.

A sharp intro announced that a bankrupt butcher had bitten off more than he could chew, or that a mugged dentist was looking down in the mouth. Keep it sharp, keep it light, keep it frothy!

I also discovered that uncertain incidents or newsworthy rumours, when fairly harmless and unlikely to lead to a complaint, could always be confirmed by an anonymous 'neighbour' or 'close friend'. They became good friends, ever willing to help a young reporter doing his best to make a headline out of a molehill.

These omnipresent and obliging characters are in fact closely related to 'an insider' and 'a well-informed source'—informants who can be spotted quite regularly in the daily and Sunday tabloids, particularly in stories which are safe to bend, such as show biz and speculative Royal 'exclusives'.

It was a time of learning the hallowed tabloid motto: never let the facts interfere with a good story.

My news-hunting patch was the Harold Hill council estate, then Europe's largest, which housed London's overspill familes, the parents of Darren and Tracey, with Alsatian dogs called Prince and Thunder. It was an era when the serious desperadoes from East London first began to move deep into the rustic isolation of the Essex countryside where, dripping with chunky gold jewellery and cheap aftershave, they did impersonations of Del Boy impersonating a country squire.

I would catch a bus to Harold Hill and spend at least three days a week walking around and knocking on the doors of likely news sources, from newsagents and grocers to local political party ward officials and tenants' association officials.

It was an area where finding 'news' wasn't difficult. There was always some kind-hearted soul willing to be encouraged to criticise the council, the police, the local MP or similar unprotected species.

They were days of learning that whatever was bad was good for a story; that the bigger the row, the bigger the headline and byline. The pursuit of controversy, and its exploitation, was all.

It was the reason for regular visits to local registry offices to check through the personal details listed on wedding banns. But not for happy-ever-after stories. The purpose was to look for the eighteen-year-old shop assistant marrying a man twice her age, or a mixed-race marriage, in days when they were news, or a council dustman from Harold Hill marrying a company director's daughter from an upmarket area. They all offered the ingredients of a family row which might make a page lead story.

Even notice boards in newsagents' shop windows were scanned for items for sale or services that might offer a touch of the bizarre. A good tabloid story, I was discovering, was all about putting ordinary people into extraordinary situations.

The *Romford Times* was more or less run by the news editor and subs. The editor, a Yorkshireman, seemed to spend little time in the office. His presence was acknowledged but little more. His main interest seemed to lie in the company of fellow Rotarians.

His reputation as a tabloid man wasn't much enhanced after he wrote a leader criticising local stores for not stocking a particular lead-based paint he required for his garage doors. The topic was painful enough, but the first sentence ran breathlessly on for some eighty words—a serious violation of the paper's crackling style.

My interview was one of the rare occasions when I spent more than a few minutes in conversation with him. The only other notable occasion came in response to a summons to his office where, with copy in hand, he sternly pointed out that it was most certainly not all right to spell 'all right' as 'alright'.

After I read the story, I noticed it had been written by another junior reporter who, some years later, was to become deputy editor of *The Sun*. The editor harrumphed me out of his office, telling me to make damn sure, m'boy, that I didn't make that kind of mistake.

On joining the *Romford Times* I had signed a three-year indenture agreement negotiated between local newspaper employers and the National Union of Journalists, which meant that I was obliged to sit in a classroom to study British constitution, newspaper law, economics and English language.

It was no doubt much needed, but whatever their successes, I wasn't among them. I did my best—I even bought a plastic zip-round holdall and a couple of exercise books—but it wasn't long before my eyes would begin to glaze over. I couldn't see what any of it had to do with getting a good story.

None of it, I decided, would make me a sharper reporter. I was far happier roaming Harold Hill and, later, the South Ockendon housing estate. Talking people into giving me stories seemed a lot easier and far more enjoyable.

How gloriously I might have failed the exams was never to be established. I was spared the inevitable disgrace by an unexpected turn of events shortly before I was due to sit them.

It followed a social visit to Associated Press to call on Don McNicol, whose practical support had crucially encouraged my ambition to become a reporter.

I mentioned in passing that after nearly three years on the *Romford Times* I was keen to move on. By now, at the age of nineteen, I could not only write a pretty sharp tabloid intro, but I could also play a reasonable game of snooker and darts, and hold a pint—all very necessary social skills in the nascent hack's plans for a successful tabloid career.

Don gave me the name of the news editor of the *Manchester Evening News*, a New Zealander he knew well, and suggested I make contact with him. I sent an exploratory letter, and, coincidentally, they had a vacancy.

Some weeks later, in the Fleet Street office of the *Manchester Evening News*, I was interviewed by the editor. The interview went well. I received a letter some days later offering me the job of a reporter, subject to a week's trial in the Manchester office.

With my mum and dad's best holiday suitcase, I travelled north to a cold, unwelcoming room in a massive YMCA hostel in Eccles Old Road, Salford.

The newsroom of the *Manchester Evening News*, then a broadsheet like the *Middlesex Independent* and not much more attractive in layout, had the funereal atmosphere of the British Museum. The arrival mid-morning of the lady with the tea trolley was an exhilarating diversion to the morning's monotony.

Reporters were expected to sit quietly at their desks until required by the newsdesk. It seemed a strained discipline compared to the headline-hunting freedom of the *Romford Times*, especially as this was the biggest selling newspaper outside of the *London Evening News*.

Over-animated conversation was discouraged and quietly quelled by the kind of memo a reporter—he was to become news editor on the *Daily Mirror*—received after he was seen talking to me, apparently a little too loudly. The newsroom was not, he was informed, a place for idle chatter.

I spent most of my days on the phone, working on stories and tips from freelances and stringers. Apart from the likes of the council and political and industrial correspondents, staff reporters seemed to see little of the outside world.

Dull days were followed by dull nights of little social activity due to a salary which, perhaps mercifully, kept me out of the nightclubs which were then opening up on every other street corner and building basement. I longed to know Mr Smith's and dance at Deano's and pose importantly at the Executive Club.

Such was the sad state of my social life that I willingly put my name forward to review local amateur dramatic society productions. They not only delayed the nightly misery of my YMCA digs, but each review earned me an extra thirty shillings.

It was easy money. A couple of hundred words, if that, of bland, anodyne comment to keep the producer and leading actors happy. It was the safest strategy, although on one occasion, when I expressed less than gushing praise, the producer wrote a stinging letter of complaint to the editor, accusing me of turning up drunk.

It was true that I had a drink to fortify myself for what lay ahead, and I did ask for the loo on my arrival at the church hall, but I was far from drunk, not that that condition wouldn't have been justified. There are only so many times a person can endure Gerald the bank clerk and Helen the typist in *The Murder of Maria Marten*.

The complaint, though, sent a seismic shudder through the upright frame of the news editor, a nice man with swept-back corrugated hair, who wore a bow-tie or sometimes a cravat, finished off with a cardigan and a pipe.

He accepted my indignant denial, but from that moment on, I think, he saw me as someone to keep an eye on. And I probably did my cause little good when I arrived for the early morning shift in a blood-stained shirt, the consequence of a woman throwing a beer can at my head, for a reason I can't remember, at an all-night party.

My news editor was not pleased; it was not in

keeping with the august reputation of the *Manchester Evening News*, which was jealously guarded by an editor who displayed an extraordinary dislike of all creatures south of the Watford Gap.

Two memorable leader articles advanced suggestions that the House of Commons should be moved to Manchester and that the FA Cup Final should be staged at Old Trafford rather than Wembley. At every opportunity, and even when there wasn't, the paper would proclaim that what Manchester did today, London would do tomorrow. It was unbridled xenophobia, but no doubt good for circulation.

In those days, the *Manchester Evening News* housed its genius in a huge, imposing building of Victorian splendour in Cross Street through which over the years reporters and writers of great talents had walked its ornately-panelled corridors and white-tiled stairwell.

Soon it would be bulldozed to oblivion, along with many other buildings in the immediate vicinity, to be replaced by a shopping centre designed by architects who clearly had little love for the human race.

But none of this had happened when I received a letter from Gwen, a girl I had known in Romford, and to which I responded eagerly. It led to a weekend in Manchester, the resumption of a relationship, which, in turn, led to her pregnancy, a flat above a Jewish butcher's shop in Bury Old Road, Prestwich, and, a few months later, a wedding at Bury Registry Office.

My mum turned up, drank a lot and cried a lot, and danced the night away with Norman, the paper's alcoholic political correspondent, and together they sang Cockney songs late into the night. Norman, a bachelor who lived with his mum in Oldham, was a good friend who was to die of his addiction.

Suddenly, from being a bachelor boy reporter aged

about twenty-one and with little money, I was a married man with two children—my wife already had a two-year-old daughter—with even less money. And soon it would get worse: I would be out of a job.

It happened shortly after a senior executive pulled a string or two to provide a staff job for his son. In his late twenties, he had done little other than write PR news releases for a record company. It was clear that but for his father's influence, he wouldn't have made the short list for a job.

A youthful idealism inflamed by such blatant nepotism expressed its outrage and anger to Norman and the barmaid in Sam's Chop House. With Norman's counsel, supported by the barmaid, I returned to the office emboldened by booze to dash out my resignation. It was good working-class bile and inspired what was possibly the longest resignation in newspaper history.

Some years later, I came across a copy. Its naïvety and innocence caused me to wince, but there was all the same a quiet admiration for a youth who, however misguidedly, pursued a principle. I never knew the editor's reaction. He probably filed it in the bin.

One month later, about three years after stepping off the coach from London, I cleared out my desk and departed the *Manchester Evening News* for casual shifts in the northern office of the *Daily Mirror*, a couple of blocks away in Withy Grove. The strained financial circumstances meant a move from the flat above the Jewish butcher's shop.

The proprieter, Sidney Yoffey, was a kind man who, like most Jews, adored children. His affection for my daughter Alexandra and step-daughter Janice was unfailingly expressed by stuffing slices of Kosher meat or sausage into their hands as we passed through the shop, followed by a slobbering kiss to the cheek.

With TV and suitcases precariously balanced on a pram, we moved into a spacious semi-detached house less than a mile away. In fact, we could have moved into any one of several dozen spacious semi-detached houses in that particular road.

The entire street was to be reduced to rubble some nine months later to make way for the construction of a motorway. Until then, in return for a peppercorn rent to the local council which had compulsorily purchased the houses, we had our choice.

Through the *Daily Mirror* shifts I met a freelance reporter who ran his own news agency in Southport, a genteel and geriatric seaside town some forty miles from Manchester.

On the strength of stories I was getting into the *Mirror*, I was offered a job with the agency. It was not a superior career move, but with no certainty of the casual shifts continuing on any permanent basis, it made sense to accept the offer.

As I couldn't afford rented accommodation in the town, or anywhere near the town, the Lovell family plus goldfish moved into a caravan in a farmer's field which was parked against the side of a barn to protect it against the gales of a northern winter.

Water came from a standpipe and Sunday dinners from a local pub—steak and kidney pies, and packets of crisps for pudding. The living conditions became so bad that I took Janice and Alexandra to stay temporarily with my mum and dad in Paddington. The goldfish was happy enough.

I quit the news agency for a staff job on the *Blackburn Times*, a weekly newspaper, which enabled me to pause for breath and lick my wounds. Bloodied, bruised and broke, it was time to get back to London.

The opportunity came a couple of months later

through an advertisement in the *UK Press Gazette*, a media trade magazine. A major London freelance news agency was looking for a news reporter with all-round experience. By now, aged twenty-three going on forty-five, I had all-round experience to spare.

Chapter Four

I closed the caravan door and travelled to Central London to meet the agency proprietor, a small man lost in a large expensive overcoat who drove a big car. He was, in the vernacular, a sharp operator, good at negotiating exclusive syndication deals, and happy to tell you how he pulled them off.

His agency, the North London News Agency, was based in converted shop premises in Hornsey, North London, a finishing school for many a national newspaper reporter. It had one function: to beat its rival, the Fleet Street News Agency, at any cost, financial or human. It was to be my first experience of the chaotic pace of Fleet Street newspapers.

The agency's stock in trade was hard news stories from six-paragraph multiple car crashes, plus pictures, to the blood and gore of brutal murders, plus pictures. The more sensational material would be syndicated overseas.

Two unlikely key players were the freelance photographers whose pictures were sold through the agency. They were both extremely professional and experienced operators. They were also, in their different ways, quite crazy.

One was known as Dingo, and the other, probably the crazier of the two, was Elgar. He was a tall, thin, hawk-nosed individual, who, in his well-worn gaberdine raincoat, looked like a hard-up rent collector. He drove a clapped-out car kept together by rust and string.

Dingo, on the other hand, dressed and acted like a high-rolling swell: mohair overcoat, expensive suits and ostentatious jewellery. In keeping with his image, his car was a big three-litre tank.

The rivalry between Elgar and Dingo was as intense as that between the two news agencies. They both 'earwigged' the emergency services on the FM waveband for information on incidents from road accidents and fires to serious crime, to which they would race to be first on the scene.

Of course, the authorities were very much aware of the antics of the likes of Elgar and Dingo, but they could do little to thwart them. Their best strategy was to transmit bogus information, await the arrival of freelances and then give them an official warning.

But a reprimand would do nothing to deter Elgar. Whatever it took to get the information he would do it. He wouldn't hesitate to impersonate a police officer and phone a local hospital or fire station for details of location or identity. His audacity was reinforced by a sound knowledge of police-speak and the police system, which invariably guaranteed success.

To Elgar and Dingo, all was fair in the freelance war, when money and reputations were on the line. They did it to prove they were sharp enough to outwit the system. It gave a challenging sharpness to their lives, even when they were relaxing.

One night, in a Chinese restaurant in Islington, Elgar demanded to see the manager, claiming that he was a local council food inspector. Was the manager aware that, under a particular section of the Restaurant Food Act 1967, there should be a certain number of prawns with all prawn dishes and why were there fewer than that number with his prawn dish? It got him an extra portion of prawns.

In another staged incident, Elgar rushed for the exit of a major department store while Dingo, in hot pursuit, shouted to onlookers, urging them to catch the 'thief'.

An heroic passer-by did just that, and a minor scuffle followed. But Dingo claimed the wrong man had been caught while Elgar heatedly claimed that his overcoat had been torn beyond repair.

In fact, it had been deliberately torn before the drama was staged. But, they claimed later, Elgar received a new overcoat from an apologetic management. It was part of the regular madness of a hustling world, which helped to relieve the pressures. It was the stuff of which reputations were made, and beloved of newspapermen.

Symptomatic of the lunacy of the day was the considerably more serious episode which put a well-respected London freelance in a court dock. Through unofficial channels, which later led to an internal investigation, he obtained copies of official police photographs of the victim of a particularly brutal murder.

A photographer colleague had also obtained illegal access to the room of the murder, which he photographed from every angle. The photographs, with the story, were syndicated to a German news magazine. But they were never published. The photographs were intercepted by the police and traced back to the agency.

Long angered by the intrusive recklessness of London-based freelances, and no doubt as a warning shot to the press at large, the freelance was prosecuted, found guilty and heavily fined. He died a short while later of a brain tumour.

Those days, which gave me my first taste of national newspapers, came to an end after about eighteen months, through an incident involving my mongrel dog, Lucky—a small long-haired ragbag of a mutt who looked the same both ends.

He was an intelligent dog who enjoyed working the occasional late shift with me. He was happy to sleep anywhere, in the office or car, and his presence was hardly noticed.

It would have remained that way but for an invitation by a colleague for a late-night spin around the West End of London in his new Mini-Cooper. It proved too much of a hair-raising experience for Lucky who, completely out of canine character, did a runner through an open rear window while the car was waiting at a set of traffic lights.

We spent some time, more time than we ought, vainly touring the streets. The incident reached the ears of the proprietor. I was called to his office to be told that it was time I followed Lucky's example and got lost.

For the record, the wonder dog miraculously turned up at my parents' home, where my family was temporarily living, a couple of weeks later.

A 100% Greater London Council mortgage acquired for the family a two-bedroomed bungalow in Rainham, Essex, just a few miles from Romford, and from where I had departed northwards a little over five years earlier.

From a sparsely-furnished room, I copied the example of Dingo and Elgar and began 'earwigging' for a couple of months, so desperate was the financial situation, before returning to the *Romford Times* for a brief spell.

I also began filing story memos to the daily and Sunday papers, including *The People*, then a broadsheet with a reputation for major investigations, but now a downmarket tabloid more in the sewer than the gutter.

A freelance reporter, who was laid on by *The People* to check out a particular story memo I had submitted, came to see me. A friendship developed, he arranged for me to work with him as a witness on potentially dodgy stories, and a news agency partnership was formed.

His asset was his contacts with *The People*. Mine was a breezeblock-built shed measuring about six feet by ten feet at the end of an overgrown garden. Rusting garden tools were cleared out and cobwebs brushed away, and we added a coat of white paint, a couple of second-hand desks and a telephone to transform the garden shed into an office.

There was also another major development to family circumstances. I became the father of a son—a handsome, very lovable boy called Toby.

The journalistic tactics of this garden shed enterprise fell somewhere between Bonnie and Clyde and Barnum and Bailey.

We mugged dozens of weekly newspapers for the faintest whiff of a story which, with a sprinkling of stardust, could be creatively transformed into an exclusive for one of the tabloids.

The main market, though, through my colleague's already established contacts, was *The People*, which was then nudging the *News of the World* as the biggest selling popular Sunday in the country.

At least a dozen 'offered exclusive memos', based on local newspaper stories, would be filed weekly to the newsdesk. It would be a bad week if at least one of our exclusive stories didn't make the paper. By then I was also being 'laid on' to handle stories submitted by other freelances.

For the first time in my life, I was making real money. I was able to buy an overnight suitcase, a travelling kit and an executive-style briefcase—and I could afford to exchange my former GPO-owned bullnosed Morris van for a saloon car with four seats and a radio that worked.

I was booking into star-rated hotels in towns and cities throughout the South and the Midlands. I was eating in restaurants with three-foot-high menus, with knives and forks all over the place, and ordering wine I couldn't pronounce. And it was all on expenses. I had stumbled into paradise.

It was a happiness crowned by my first national newspaper byline, in *The People*. The ecstasy can be likened perhaps to an unknown actor suddenly seeing his name up in lights over a West End theatre. I remember the story well, and the victims. And to their memories I apologise.

Centre stage was a seventy-five year old pensioner, whom I billed as a 'heartbreaking Romeo' for 'spurning the love' of his fiancée, Mabel, aged seventy, for a younger woman—all of sixty-five. It was a fun-poking story which made a page lead, and earned the congratulations of the news editor who called me to his office to confirm my promising stardom.

The byline meant, he told me, that I had crossed the 'dividing line'—I had joined the paper's elite team of bylined freelances. I walked out of the office with my ego in overdrive.

But the story made fools of those people, particularly the elderly man and the woman he rejected. They were humiliated, and no doubt many laughs were had at their expense, but that was of no concern to me. What I did was what tabloid newspaper reporters did. It was the way it was. All I knew, and all I cared about, was the professional recognition it had given me and the money that came with it.

For the first time, it gave me a financial security that I had only dreamed of. I didn't give a second thought to whatever I was asked to do. You want me to jump? Sure, sir. How high? You want me to turn someone over? Be delighted!

Business became so good that the family was able to move out of the two-bedroomed bungalow and into a four-bedroomed detached house in the upmarket commuter town of Witham, near Chelmsford. The Jack-the-lad image was reinforced by a 3.4 S Jaguar— second-hand but in good nick.

There was also an office relocation: to two rooms above a sausages-and-mash café on the outskirts of Romford town centre. It wasn't a class act, but it was a cut above the garden shed.

My colleague had by now left the agency—and his wife—for the love of a newsdesk secretary. In his place came a local paper reporter, whose tabloid skills would take him to the staff of *The People*, and a freelance photographer who worked on our picture stories.

Exclusive picture stories to the dailies were a lucrative source of income. Some were inspired by magazine cartoons—the kind which could be easily transformed into 'real life' situations—such as the cartoon which showed a proud angler standing in front of his prize catches—a bent bicycle wheel, a battered kettle and a wellington boot—in wall-mounted display cases.

In return for a few quid and a couple of pints, a local pub regular agreed to play the part of the angler—a bar-room 'star' willing to be made famous for fifteen minutes could usually be found—and with his photograph went an exclusive story about the world's worst angler.

Other picture stories were inspired by news items tucked away down page, such as the announcement by a brewery that it was closing down a pub. The publican agreed to dress up as a vicar, with regulars as pall-bearers, to bury the last barrel of beer in the pub garden, complete with its own 'RIP' headstone.

Another picture story, which ended up as an exclusive in one of the daily tabloids, featured a businessman who said in a local paper story that he was praying for good weather for a VIP barbecue as part of wedding anniversary celebrations. Surprisingly, he agreed to dress up as an Indian and do a dance in the garden to please the sun god.

I had no scruples about this kind of strip cartoon news. I saw it, not as news, but as pure slapstick which was fun to do, caused no harm and helped pay the mortgage.

All the same, I kept our creative efforts well away from *The People*, the agency's biggest source of income. I couldn't risk 'stunting' a story just in case it backfired. That would have been disastrous, particularly if it resulted in a legal complaint.

But that is precisely what happened in a moment of carelessness when a 'creatively projected' picture story was offered to *The People*. It was bought and published, with disastrous consequences.

The star of the show was Milly the goat. She was the pet of a woman who, her weekly newspaper announced, had opened a health food shop where fresh goat's milk was available courtesy of Milly. In those days, when health food was in its infancy and something of a consumer novelty, it was a news item.

A short while later, I was on the phone asking the owner that if goat's milk was good for one's health, and if one's state of health was important to sexual performance, did it follow that Milly's milk could improve jaded sex lives?

She obligingly agreed that, put that way, it probably could. By the end of our phone conversation, she consented to a picture session involving Milly and several of her woman customers.

The photographer arrived to take photographs of Milly tied to a lamp-post while her owner, sitting on a stool, pretended to milk her. Completing the shot was a queue of housewives, all friends of the owner, waiting for their pots and pans to be filled with the aphrodisiacal delights of Milly's milk.

The following Sunday a photograph of Milly and the housewives was published in *The People*. But the following Tuesday, the beginning of a Sunday newspaper's working week, the newsdesk's telephones apparently came close to melt-down, with furious protests from some very angry husbands claiming they were greatly embarrassed by the story and photograph, which implied they were not quite up to the mark.

They claimed that their wives had been led to believe they were taking part in some harmless publicity to promote their friend's health food shop. The phone calls were promptly followed by solicitors' letters threatening legal action.

The photographer and I were summoned separately to *The People* to be grilled by the office lawyer, a very shrewd old bird straight out of Dickens, who wore half-moon glasses on the end of his nose and wing collars. Assisted by an associate editor, he had the task of getting the newspaper out of trouble with the least possible damage to its name and profits.

In that kind of situation, particularly for a vulnerable freelance, the goat's milk of human kindness was in short supply. A staff reporter could survive that kind of upset, but the dispensable freelance had little protection.

There was no defence I could offer. The associate editor, long in the tooth, knew it was a stunt which had backfired. I had committed the cardinal sin for a tabloid freelance. I had been caught out. It was goodnight, Vienna.

After some three years of lucrative exclusives with *The People*, I was out in the cold. That night, in the office pub, aptly nicknamed The Stab in the Back, and used by all the Mirror Group newspapers' editorial staff, my predicament caused a lot of laughs and little sorrow.

Overnight, my contact with *The People* ceased. The daily calls between the agency and the newsdesk came to an abrupt end. All my eggs had been in one newspaper's basket, and now they were all over my face.

It led rapidly to the break-up of the news agency. My marriage was going much the same way. My prospects, on all fronts, looked bleak. I could no longer afford the mortgage, the office rent or the Jag.

While considering life's options in Fleet Street's Press Club, I met by chance a former daily tabloid newspaper executive who some months earlier, and while very drunk, had assaulted a colleague with an empty champagne bottle during the night shift.

It led to his dismissal and a new life in Spain, in the historic city of Segovia, north east of Madrid, where his wife gave English lessons to wealthy Spaniards while he did little, other than enjoy good wine and suckling pig, and play a pinball machine in a local bar.

At the time, a new life in the sun seemed like a good idea.

In a hired transit van, loaded to the gunwales with bags and baggage, with three children and a twelve-stone Newfoundland dog called Leo, we headed for Dover on the first leg of a journey with only the destination a certainty; where we would live in Spain wasn't, nor was the question of what I would do to turn an honest peseta.

Also in the transit van, giving me some reassurance, was a well-hidden £9,000—the proceeds from the sale of our house. I smuggled the money out of the country due to a currency control law which at that time restricted the amount of money that could be legally taken out of the country.

We spent a couple of months culturally acclimatising in a village called Palazuelos, a few kilometres from Segovia, before moving south to Mojacar, a fashionable enclave for Europeans in the south-east province of Almeria.

There, we bought a three-bedroomed villa, one of a row of four newly built near the main coastal road, beyond which was the beach and the Mediterranean.

It was a convenient five-minute drive from Mojacar, an ancient town of strong Moorish influence stationed on top of a small mountain range to the right, and, to the left, a five-minute drive to the fishing village of Garrucha.

It was the perfect setting, I romanticised, to write my first international mega-selling book. I set up literary shop on the villa's terraced roof, under a parasol, with a large bottle of cheap vino tinto and a packet of Ducados cigarettes—fatal to both health and flies—by my side. It was, I imagined, what John Steinbeck would have done.

After three days of dripping blood onto virgin white paper, I arrived at the decision to write an international bestseller another time. I reckoned I had plenty of time. Instead, in the bars of Mojacar, I pondered my future through a glass of cuba libre darkly.

In this way, I came across a cabaret of characters, including Dan the Man, an upper-class Brit who, behind locked doors, wore women's clothes; Franz, a powerfully-built German psycho, long disowned by his wealthy family, who spent his days planning elaborate drug deals and beating up his wife; Max, a gifted but perpetually drunk artist who wanted to draw me in the nude; and Salvatori, a homosexual Sicilian-American who ran Sal's Bar without legal documentation.

The son of a member of the Mafiosa in Trenton, New Jersey, who had allegedly been prominent in Chicago during Prohibition, Sal suggested I wrote his biography. With nothing better in mind, I agreed.

But a major problem soon arose. He couldn't discuss his relationship with his father, whom he blamed for his homosexuality, without breaking down in a torrent of tears. The slightest probing question seemed to upset him so badly that he would be unable to continue.

The solution, he suggested, lay in a brief trip to Kenitra in Morocco where, among friends living on the

US naval base, he could relax. As I hadn't been to Morocco, and the cost would be minimal, I agreed. It was to be one of those times in life that remain vividly etched in the memory for ever.

We caught the Algerciras ferry to Tangier and booked in to what must have been the most popular hotel in the city. A million flies couldn't be wrong.

That night, as we sat at a pavement café in the Medina finishing a succulent meal of kebabs, Sal, who had been getting progressively smashed on hashish and red wine, suddenly declared that he loved me. In a dramatic demonstration of that love, he spreadeagled his left hand and, in the same instant, plunged a kebab skewer through it and into the table.

It was very dramatic, very Sicilian and, surprisingly, produced very little blood. I explained, as gently as possible, that I couldn't reciprocate his feelings; that it really wasn't my preference. Sal said nothing, but he looked as though he was in pain.

A few moments later, he called for the bill and, with a paper napkin wrapped round his hand, he manfully disappeared into the night. The subject never came up again.

The next day we drove to Kenitra to enjoy the open-house hospitality of an army base dentist and his family. Throughout my stay, his wife seemed uncomfortable in my presence, as if she couldn't quite make me out. I think she thought I was in Sal's team, but she couldn't be sure.

Despite my best efforts to encourage Sal, his interest in the book had fallen away completely. In unhappy, sulking mood, he declined an invitation from the dentist to the base's 150th anniversary celebrations of the founding of the US marines.

It was the kind of predictable Hollywood-style event

that only the Americans can stage, awash with General Paton look-alikes and Omar Sharif sheiks saluting Berkely Babe military bands.

By midnight, the top table guests had left, and the banquet hall was now littered with pockets of hard-drinking marines and their debris. It had been an enjoyable night and would have ended that way but for the comments of a marine of the Neanderthal platoon, who, passing the table at which I was sitting alone, made a critical comment about limeys.

I didn't actually hear the comment, but the dentist's wife, sitting with the rest of the party at an adjoining table, did, and she was quick to let me know that it had been very insulting of the British. She said it in a tone which challenged my patriotism.

Although I hadn't heard what he had said, I had seen the marine with no neck, his knuckles trailing along the floor, rejoin his friends at the bar. In the absence of a credible alternative to get me out of the situation, I rose from the table in my best John Wayne style and walked as confidently as the circumstances would allow towards the group of marines.

As if on cue, several moved to one side, leaving me face to face with the son of Godzilla. We both knew what was about to happen. Or, rather, what he was about to do to me. I drew a fist back to throw my first, best and probably last punch. But it didn't connect.

In that instant, a fist at the end of an arm that came lunging over my shoulder hit the marine full in the face. He crumpled to the floor.

Suddenly, I was in the middle of a riot. Tables and chairs were overturned and women ran for the exit as white-helmeted military police moved in with drawn truncheons.

My parting memory was of the dentist pulling

me frantically away, pleading: 'Please, Terry, for my sake . . . .' Straightjacketed in his arms and being dragged to safety, I put on a fine show of being willing to take on every marine in the place.

I had no idea who threw the punch that probably saved my life, but, like the seventh cavalry, it arrived in the nick of time.

A day or two later, after Sal went looking for drugs he had apparently buried during a previous trip and now couldn't find, we returned to Mojacar, with no further mention of the book. All in all, it had been A Bad Day at Black Rock.

If there was one bright spot in those days it came early one morning as I strolled along the beach with the sun rising in a sky of stunning colour. I came across a dead baby porpoise, its eyes devoured by nests of flies.

It seemed such an undignified end, so I dragged it by the tail into the water, expecting it to float out to sea and sink. But in Mediterranean water without a tide it went no further. I waded in and took it out as far as I could and swam back to the beach. I looked out from the beach and saw no sign of it

Later that day, after midday, I went out onto the porch of the villa and, looking out to the sea, I saw a school of porpoises rollercoasting through the water, surprisingly close, I thought, to the beach.

A neighbour, a farmer working the land, saw them too. I'm not sure why, but I told him about the baby porpoise and what had happened. He said the porpoise's family had come to thank me. I didn't believe it, but it was a nice thought.

They were bizarre days, and stupid days. Franz said he would beat up his wife (I heard a couple of years later that she had died of a brain tumour) unless I agreed to drive him to Madrid for a drugs deal arranged to take place outside the American Express office.

We booked into a pension, and, in my room, I laid on the bed and phoned someone I knew in England. I forgot the time and the bill mounted up. The next morning, Franz didn't have enough to meet the cost. He had to cut into the money set aside for the deal.

He couldn't make up the shortfall in time and the deal fell through. Franz was like an enraged bull throughout the return journey to Mojacar. And he refused to pay for the petrol.

During many months of doing nothing, apart from spending money that was quickly running out, I doggedly pursued life in the bars of Mojacar. There were too many nights of driving drunkenly from the town to the villa, and sleeping through days of monotonous routine.

Early one morning, after a night of alcohol, my luck ran out. With Franz by my side, I drove out of Mojacar and down the mountain road for a disco on the beach. I took a bend too fast, and the wheels skidded on a carpet of stone and gravel washed down by heavy rains. The car came to a halt on the edge of a precipice, and for a second or two seemed to remain stationary. I thought we were safe, until we slowly toppled into the darkness below.

I was knocked unconscious on the way down. The car came to rest upside-down on the roof of a small stone dwelling where a peasant family kept a pig. The car had fallen about sixty feet.

When I came round there was a strong smell of petrol. Franz was able to unwind a rear window through which we crawled to safety. I suffered nothing worse than a cut head, and Franz some minor cuts and a fractured rib, although the next day he collapsed, apparently through delayed shock.

The car had landed on its roof, with no more than perhaps two feet clearance between the roof and the dashboard. We had both been thrown into the back of the car. If we had been wearing seatbelts, strapping us to the front seats, we would have been killed. Of that I have no doubt. Our survival was a miracle.

The next morning I returned to survey the damage. The local kids had already moved in virtually stripping the car, a Renault 16TS which I bought in Madrid, down to its chassis.

It was so badly damaged that the insurance company claimed that it could not have been possible for two men to survive the fall. In refusing to pay my claim, the company argued, mistakenly, that I must have pushed the car off the mountain road to collect the insurance money.

I was also informed by a straight-faced Guardia Civil officer that the owner of the pig was threatening to take legal action because of the alleged stress the animal had suffered.

This incident marked the lowest point of some twelve months in Spain—months of particularly self-centred folly, when money and time were squandered by a young man who looked for nothing but the next entertaining distraction, with scant regard for a marriage that had now come to an end.

Even for the sake of the children, I was unable to bring myself to make the genuine effort necessary for its salvage. I suppose I had married too young and in the wrong circumstances. In my confusion and bitter-ness, I had not been able to make the commitment marriage demands.

Finally, with just enough money to cover the short-term cost of temporary accommodation in a mobile home just outside London, we left Spain and returned to England.

It was in the garden of a friend's home where I told Janice, Alexandra and Toby that I couldn't stay. I tried to explain why their mother and I found it impossible to stay together.

Toby followed me to the pavement and looked on as I got into my car. I saw him in the rearview mirror, standing there on the pavement, watching me drive away. He was about seven years old. I still weep when I think of the unhappiness I caused my children that day.

Chapter Five

During my lost twelve months in Spain, there had been some executive editorial changes on *The People*, which offered an opportunity to re-establish contact as a freelance. I was ready to work all hours, not just to pay the fine imposed by HM Customs & Excise for smuggling the house sale proceeds out of the UK, but to help smother the guilt and sadness I felt in leaving my children.

The newsroom gave me an anchor, a place of belonging, and I was happy to work long hours. The bylines resumed, and I enjoyed the results, but in those days newspaper unions reigned supreme and my enthusiasm was not welcomed by a few of the more militant reporters, which included, of course, the chapel (union) officials.

A willingness to work on any story at any time condemned me in their eyes as a 'newsdesk man'. Their criticisms couldn't have concerned me less. I enjoyed the job and I needed the money. I wasn't swayed by the hypocrisy of their politics—fat cat reporters who were paid tremendous salaries and expenses and who, for ever whingeing, did all they could to avoid justifying them.

A couple of reporters expressed their disapproval of my presence in the newsroom in the bluntest terms. One blocked my path in the newsroom to tell me in very clear language to return to Romford. The other, in a fit of anger, actually threw some punches at me as I sat at a desk because I had been called in to stand up a story his time-wasting tactics were in danger of killing.

If anything, I felt flattered. I reckoned that if I was riling them that much, then whatever I was doing I was doing right. Within about twelve months of freelancing full time for *The People*, a vacancy occurred. I got the job, and did cartwheels down Fleet Street.

Now I was bomb-proof, a member of an exclusive club of reporters protected by the dinosaur brawn of the National Union of Journalists, who couldn't be sacked for anything less than shooting the editor in front of at least three witnesses. It gave me the security I desperately needed.

The messenger boy who couldn't write his own job application had finally made it to the staff of one of Fleet Street's top Sunday tabloids. It also doubled as a holiday camp, where a typical working week consisted of thirty-two hours often spread over four days.

It would begin on Tuesday at about 10.30 am, a day spent filling in largely bogus expenses the equivalent to the weekly wage of the average factory worker. Allowances covered generous payments for mileage, lunch, dinner, late meal, overnight accommodation, newspapers and home phone bills, and late-night taxis for subs.

The allowances were increased annually to provide a back-door way for the management to agree to new pay deals with the NUJ without being seen to do so. For that reason, expenses were considered sacrosanct. They were seen to be part of a reporter's salary and, if cut, would lead to a serious confrontation between the Father of the Chapel (the National Union of Journalists' shop steward) and the news editor.

After completing his expenses, a reporter would break for lunch at about 1pm, which until 3–3.30pm would be spent in The Stab (the office pub), a local wine bar, a restaurant or all three. His visit to the office would end by no later than 6pm. If he had been given a story, he would begin working on it the following day.

No reporter would be expected to handle more than one story a week, even if it could be wrapped up in half the time. There were a dozen ways of stretching a story out to Friday evening, and an equal number to kill it off altogether if it suited the reporter's mood. For that reason, the reporter's goodwill was often crucial to a story's success.

The general rule was to give certain reporters, particularly the troublesome ones, the kind of story they were known to enjoy, and which also guaranteed a handsome byline and expenses. That way there was a reasonable chance they would come back with a result.

The power of the NUJ and the influence of office chapels was such that *The People* newsdesk was largely ruled by consensus, as were all Fleet Street newsdesks. Every newspaper employee down to the toilet cleaner knew he was protected game, who could not be sacked without the very real risk of strike action.

Constantly vulnerable to the political caprices of the unions in days when, as ever, circulation wars were of life-or-death intensity, an editor would have sooner given away his last case of vintage wine, if not his wife, than see his paper threatened by a dispute in the newsroom or machine room.

It meant that management across the board could

not manage without the recalcitrant co-operation of piratical union officials, especially the print unions whose stranglehold on production, a constant threat to the wafer-thin profits and survival of some newspapers, precipitated the computerised revolution of the newspaper industry that almost overnight would emasculate union power.

That shift of power would return total control to a management which, long frustrated by the unions' weakening and undermining of its role, soon responded with a searching overhaul of staffing levels and general production structure. It caused widespread redundancies, including tougher working conditions which put staff morale at an all-time low. The pendulum, it seemed, had swung from one dictatorship to another.

But, until then, it was still days of wine and poseurs as the Fleet Street gravy train, unaware of the sidings just around the bend, rattled merrily along.

The People at that time enjoyed the tail-end of a reputation created by a number of notable investigations which had uncovered a number of major scandals in previous years. In some cases, a reporter would have been exposed to real danger as over many months the necessary evidence on the activities of powerful and corrupt men on both sides of the law was painstakingly obtained.

Among *The People*'s glory days coups had been the naming of the four Messina brothers as the overlords of widespread prostitution and racketeering in Soho. One of the brothers was arrested and the other three fled the country.

It exposed a drugs firm making vast profits from National Health subscriptions. Its enquiries cost *The People* £300,000 in lost advertising revenue, which, in the sixties when the story was published, was a considerable sum.

It was the first newspaper to use tape recorders in an investigation. They proved crucial in acquiring evidence that senior police officers had blackmailed petty crooks into setting up bank raids to improve the crime clear-up rate.

Amid political furore, and to the anger of senior Labour government ministers, *People* reporters also tracked down, some twenty years after the event, members of a British army patrol to prove it had been responsible for the massacre of twenty-five Malayans wrongly suspected of sheltering communist terrorists in their village.

The People also proved that the then head of Scotland Yard's Flying Squad was taking cash and holiday bribes from pornography dealers. He was jailed for five years.

It caused a public outcry—and a major investigation by the Football Association—when it was revealed that first division soccer stars were taking bribes to throw vital cup matches.

It was this area of journalism that had always attracted me. The quick-hit page leads had become predictable, while the planning and uncertainty of investigative stories in the company of a chequered range of villains offered an adrenalin-boosting challenge. I enjoyed the freedom, the self-direction and, yes, the company of some of those dodgy, bent-nosed Runyonesque characters.

I was never involved in the calibre of investigation of *The People*'s glory years, but, for the record, during those early days I posed as a drug addict in London's Soho to name dealers in a Chinese heroin racket; as a commercial agent to expose lottery-rigging by soccer clubs; as an ex-con to name the operators behind an illegal immigrants route via Holland into the UK; and as a show biz agent to name crooked working men clubs' officials who were taking bribes in return for booking acts.

I exposed a child pornography ring; a high-class brothel in Kensington where overseas students were working to supplement their government grants; a political scandal involving a young male prostitute; and a paedophile ring kidnapping children as young as four years of age.

There were many more—more than I wish to recall. But you will get the drift. They would have probably been dismissed as lightweight sensationalism by the old-time investigative reporters, and they would be right.

They would have been equally scornful of the Sunday tabloids' bi-annual 'scandalous sex dossier' which exposes, with the active encouragement of reporters posing as man and wife, the activities of the sexually depraved to titillate the appetites of the like-minded.

No less manipulated and duped are the victims in tabloid 'buy-ups', the much-criticised practice of cheque-book journalism. I negotiated a number of these, some big, some small, and they all meant one thing: the person who signed an exclusive contract after waking one morning to find he or she had become unwittingly involved in a headline scandal was bought body, soul and quote.

Once the newspaper has paid the piper—or the lawyer, who in the company of his peers no doubt haughtily condemns the immorality of cheque-book journalism—it can twist a story any way it wishes, something the unsuspecting punter, with his head full of pound notes, often lives to regret. A 'buy-up' is a practice appreciated by the reporter on the newspaper which has made the successful bid because it also guarantees an easy ride and a billboard-size byline.

The rest of the pack is left, like carrion crows, to scavenge where it might in desperate efforts to equal the successful newspaper's 'exclusive' revelations. They will do anything to produce a 'spoiler'—to the delirious delight of the editor if achieved—which is then trumpeted as the real inside exclusive. In the middle of it all are the family and relatives whose lives are devastated by the news-hunting tactics of the tabloid pack.

It was a world in which the bad and bizarre, freaks, crooks and oddballs were the norm. And I confess to enjoying it all. I saw them as good days then because they were better, more prosperous, days than I had ever known. Whatever was necessary to get a story was all right my me.

The greater the challenge, the greater my determination, driven by a turbo-charged ego, to pull it off. The more difficult the story, the more I wanted to prove I could stand it up. I felt I had a reputation to maintain and I wanted to show the world what a star I was. There was a constant need to prove myself, an immature attitude that couldn't back down even in the face of physical pain.

Once, in the bar of an Aberdeen hotel, knee-deep in Americans and Jack Daniels malt whisky, I accepted a wager to burn a hole with a cigarette through a dollar note. It seemed easy enough—until the American wrapped the dollar note around my wrist. I won the bet—a bottle of highland malt whisky—and the scar remains with me as a permanent memento of the madness of it all.

I did it to gain the confidence of oil-rig workers in digging, along with two other reporters, for any kind of sensational material to justify a Gold Rush-type series on the North Sea oil bonanza. They were destructive days and drunken nights.

I countered criticisms of tabloid newspaper tactics by claiming that it was all 'in the interests of the public', at least on so-called investigative stories. But it was all nonsense. I was no more concerned with defending the interests of the public than the newspaper executives who pulled my strings. The tabloid hack is like a bullet. He is placed in the cylinder and the trigger is pulled. He is an unthinking and uncaring missile targeted to rip people apart.

He cannot risk questioning the morality or meaning of what he does. If he searched for honest answers, and acted on them, he would put himself out of business. I believe that many hacks end up on the bottle because, deep down, they are unable to cope any longer with all the sick junk in their lives.

Three years after joining the staff of *The People*, I was appointed to its executive ranks. I came to understand at first hand the political ways of the management structure. The experience was to prove a time of considerable learning—about myself and my executive colleagues. When I applied for the vacancy of northern news editor in the Manchester office, I didn't think I'd get it. But I needed to get off the road. I was feeling tired and burned out from spending too much time in hotels and bars. And things seemed to be getting a little bit out of control.

After meeting a contact in a city-centre pub one lunchtime, I finally staggered off long after closing time to awake later that evening behind a tarpaulin screening a nearby building. I had lain down on a pile of scaffolding poles and fallen asleep.

Several months later, I came round one night in a hospital cubicle, bloodied but neatly stitched with an arm in a sling, after drunkenly driving my car into the rear of a van conveniently parked outside Paddington General Hospital in Harrow Road, Paddington.

It had happened while on my way home from a story, after that legendary one drink too many. The ambulance driver, who helped to stretcher me out of the back of the van through whose doors I had been catapulted, recognised me when I returned to the hospital late the following morning. He stopped me to say that when he saw the condition of the two vehicles and my unconscious body, he was sure I was dead.

I was lucky to escape prosecution for drunken driving—and only did so because I hauled myself off the cubicle bed and walked out of the hospital to the safety of my parents' home nearby.

There was actually a police officer waiting nearby, presumably to breathalyse me, and whose hand I expected to feel on my shoulder at any instant, as I walked in the opposite direction. Fortunately, I knew the hospital exit routes well. As an accident-prone, short-trousered kid with a snotty nose I had spent quite a bit of time in the casualty ward.

But there was another driving incident, which was certainly badly timed, occurring the day before my appointment in Manchester was announced.

Late for a meeting, I was stopped for speeding near Buckingham Palace—I should have known better in that area—and breathalysed. I was actually tested twice as the first test proved negative. In fact I had had very little more than a pint to drink that evening, but I had eaten hardly at all that day. In any event, I couldn't complain: the twelve-month ban I later received at

Bow Street magistrate's court was poetic justice.

The editor, a gruff walrus of a man, took it well. I was expecting to be told that there had been a change of heart over my appointment. But I don't think he even reprimanded me. Perhaps he knew what I was heading into.

So, for the second time, I packed my bags and headed north to Manchester. This time with a new family: my wife Sue, and son Sam, just two years old.

The northern editor was a quiet, gentle man who kept an open wine cabinet in his office and a pet ferret at home. He was a man who sought a peaceful life at almost any cost, which was, I think, often high.

He was essentially a solid top table sub, who had been the paper's northern deputy editor, until the departure of the editor, a considerably more extrovert character whose hard-drinking misdemeanours finally led to his dishonourable discharge.

The northern office had apparently been making little contribution to the paper, and the editor's departure was followed, for other reasons, by that of the northern news editor, which created the vacancy I was about to fill.

There had been considerable opposition among the northern staff to the post being filled by someone from London. The NUJ chapel officials had firmly let it be known that the position should be filled by someone in the Manchester office; by someone who had some knowledge of the north.

They weren't aware that I had worked on the *Manchester Evening News*, a fact that settled that issue. The editor's over-ruling of their demand was not well received, particularly as their candidate—a militant chapel official—was well known for his support of the principle of generous expenses.

By the end of the first week, it had become clear that there was going to be little enthusiasm for work in general or support for me in particular. I gathered I threatened a well-established, self-governing routine which dictated its own pace and results.

I responded in the only way I knew: I brought in freelances, keen for the glory and the cash, at every opportunity. I also began to do the unthinkable: I queried, and even cut, reporters' expenses.

It was not unusual in those early days to see an indignant reporter, expenses in hand, marching behind a chapel official into the office of an editor who was putting on years daily. There were also times when we both knew a story had been killed by wilful neglect, and I would send a reporter on an overnight job to Hull—the ultimate penalty.

These tactics were never ideal solutions. In fact, they weren't solutions at all. But in days when the news editor had little, if any, power, and with senior executives rarely willing to become involved in issues beyond their own personal interests, there were no easy or unmessy answers. A request to the reporters to be nice lads and play the game wasn't an option.

The tension during those months reached a new height when a mandatory chapel meeting was held to hear a complaint by a reporter who, failing to stand up a story, was humiliated, he claimed, because I shouted at him.

The evidence for the prosecution was topped up by a sports reporter, claiming to be passing the newsroom at the time, who said in all his twenty-five years in newspapers he had never heard a reporter spoken to in that way.

At the chapel's kangaroo court, which I was

forbidden by the London editor to attend, the chapel's guilty verdict—very much a foregone conclusion—earned me the infamous distinction of being the first news editor in newspaper history to be 'branched'.

It meant that the incident would be reported to the local branch of the National Union of Journalists. If a similar incident occurred, I was warned, industrial action could follow.

The pressures were not eased by certain executive colleagues who were obviously keen to do little to smooth my path. I learned later that an executive in London had mischieviously made it known that I had been sent to Manchester to 'sort out' the reporters.

It wasn't true. I had been given no such brief, but the executive, who well knew the problems in the Manchester office and reporters' opposition to a London import, also knew that nothing was more likely to whip up their hostility.

In all seriousness, another executive advised me to take one particularly difficult reporter out of the office and hit him. It was advice I ignored. The chapel, with the powerful backing of the Manchester branch, would have had me hung, drawn and quartered, which, I suspected, was the object behind the executive's advice.

The worst incident of all, I think, involved yet another executive colleague who, well known for his contacts with senior officers in Manchester police force, invited me to have a social drink later with a detective chief superintendent.

The executive had known that we were investigating the activities of certain CID officers who, it was alleged, were selling back onto the streets drugs confiscated during police raids.

For some weeks, I had been sending a freelance

reporter into clubs in Moss Side, an area known for its widespread drug-dealing, and a regular target for drugs squad officers. The reporter, dressed like something the dog had dragged in, and wired up with a tape recorder, had got enough, in my opinion, to stand the story up.

The executive, who knew that everything was about wrapped up, said that the detective chief superintendent would be very happy to 'mark my card'. Trustingly, and stupidly, I agreed.

In a pub near to his office, the detective chief superintendent, with a detective sergeant by his side; allowed a brief time of social small-talk to pass before telling me that he wanted the tapes and the transcripts to be handed over to him.

I stormed out of the pub, realising I had been set up. The following morning, before anyone else arrived in the newsroom, I tore into the executive. Whatever he did, or whoever he spoke to later, it was enough to sabotage the investigation. That incident ended our executive relationship for the rest of my time in Manchester.

I was learning a great deal about the executive game, and the main lesson was that if the reporters weren't going to trip over themselves to help me get stories into the paper, my executive colleagues weren't going to bust a gut either.

It seemed to me that they were all looking after their own corners, and to hell with the newspaper. It was the beginning of a frustration and anger that never eased. I realised that if I was going to do the job the way I knew it should be done—and that was my intention—then I was in for a hard battle.

There were many times when a life on the road with rogues and crooks seemed like a walk in the park compared to the frustrations of the northern news-desk. But I was too arrogant, self-confident and bloody-minded to back down. I was determined to get the best stories into the paper, even if I had only the office cleaner on my side.

Between cutting expenses, the attractions of Hull on a wet Friday night, and the support of a small number of freelances, changes started to happen. Northern stories were making more impact in the paper. Three reporters decided their future lay elsewhere and their resignations enabled me to bring in some new, more energetic blood.

The appearance of northern stories in the paper became an increasingly regular event, to a degree that saw the northern office not only filling its own editions, but also grabbing page leads in the southern editions.

This created its own problems. It was a development not welcomed by certain executives in London. They didn't care for an invasion of their pages by the northern office, which was supposed to be there as second fiddle to the mighty London operation. Politically, it was seen by some as a provocative statement.

Naïvely, I didn't see it that way. Besides, I didn't place the northern-based stories. Which stories went into the southern editions was decided by the London editor at the Saturday morning editorial conference. All the same, I came to learn that the appearance of too many northern stories in the paper was considered out of order. It was too threatening.

It led to a variety of crude tactics to kill major stories on the northern news schedule, which invariably followed the same routine. An executive would phone on a Friday evening to raise queries on stories which had been wired to London at least twenty-four hours earlier.

That the queries were often superfluous wasn't the point; it was that they couldn't be resolved in time for the story to be published. As a result, the executive would insist on holding the story over ostensibly for the following week's paper, but that was the kiss of death. Held-over stories, overtaken by fresh events, became stale news, and rarely survived.

I dealt with this tactic in the same way that I had responded when the two reporters in London expressed their disapproval of my keenness for stories: I took it as a compliment, and worked even harder. I told myself not to get mad, but to get even.

It was the wrong attitude. I should have gone to other more senior executives for guidance. But by then it was too late, I told myself. A couple of months after arriving in Manchester, I had gone to an executive to tell him that I wanted to see the London editor to discuss the situation. He advised me not 'to rock the boat'.

I accepted bad advice, which helped to develop a siege mentality—a sense of isolation that there was no one to turn to. I felt no threat or concern about the rival papers. They were never an issue. The dangers seemed to come from within my own paper.

There came a time when the northern editor, who had been unwillingly hauled into too many of my battles, said that I was 'too hard', and that may have been true. But it wasn't the way I had planned it to be.

When we first met in the London office, before my appointment was announced, I told him I wouldn't go to Manchester with 'guns blazing'. I meant it, but within three months it was obvious that I wasn't going to survive without some heavy artillery.

Three years after moving to Manchester, although by now the northern office had established a new standing, I continued pursuing, with or without London's blessing, all and every story, and even one or two in Los Angeles. I believed that getting results was my best protection against those whom I suspected would delight in my downfall.

The London editor had transformed *The People* from an ailing broadsheet into a tabloid, and so successfully that it threatened the 4 million-plus circulation of the Sunday tabloid market leader, the *News of the World*.

He was also one of the few tabloid editors who respected the authority of the Press Council. In fact, a complaint to the Press Council was said to cause him greater concern than a writ for libel.

In a space of several months, two investigations under my direction came in for public criticism—and the first through the Press Council. It upheld a complaint against the publication of an investigation into parents' allegations that teenage girls living in a hospital for the mentally handicapped were allowed so much sexual freedom that an increasing number were becoming pregnant.

The allegations were substantiated by parents' affidavits and the evidence of a female reporter who was able to get a job in the hospital.

The Press Council complaint came not from the hospital, staff or parents, but through a mental health charity which argued that the sexual licence was positive in helping the girls' emotional development. It also decried the undercover tactic.

The Press Council agreed, and upheld the complaint—a decision which, I was soon to hear, caused the editor to turn every known shade of purple.

It caused him far greater concern than the public wigging *The People* received from a judge at Manchester Crown Court.

He rounded on the paper at the end of a trial based on the evidence of an investigation by the northern office into allegations of bribery involving dog show judges. Its publication was based on sworn affidavits by dog breeders and tape-recorded admissions by the judges that bribes had been offered and accepted.

At the end of the hearing, the judge, after directing the jury to acquit the dog show judges, strongly criticised *The People* for using the dog breeders to 'entrap' the judges. Predictably, his comments received wide coverage in the press.

There was, though, a third story which reached neither the Press Council nor the courts. In fact, it was never published, but its consequences caused such a confrontation in the editor's office that it signalled the beginning of the end of my days on the northern newsdesk.

The story, the result of an investigation over many weeks, centred on a pregnancy advisory clinic in the north which was declaring negative pregnancy tests to be positive, and then arranging for bogus abortions to be carried out at a private nursing home—in which it had a major financial interest.

A total of ten women reporters, some freelance but mostly from local newspapers, agreed to be wired up with tape recorders and call at the clinic for pregnancy tests.

As part of the legal groundwork, they were all medically examined prior to their visits to the clinic. In each case, signed statements were obtained from a medical practitioner confirming they were not pregnant.

However, following the pregnancy tests, four of the

women were told they were pregnant and issued with confirmatory documentation. The claims of staff were tape recorded, as were the arrangements to send them to a particular nursing home for their 'abortions' to be carried out.

In each case, again for legal reasons, the women were examined immediately after leaving the pregnancy clinic to confirm they were not pregnant. One of the more senior and experienced women agreed to book in, again wired up, for an overnight stay in the nursing home to confirm that doctors were prepared to carry out the 'abortion'. Shortly before it was due to take place, she hurriedly left the premises.

Documentation, tape recordings and medical evidence were dossiered and sent to London. Only the showdowns with the pregnancy agency and nursing home principals remained to be done. It was a powerful story.

But the reaction from London was swift and sharp: I was summoned to the editor's office to be severely reprimanded. He wanted to know why the northern office had undertaken the investigation without the knowledge of the London newsdesk.

While the London office hadn't been officially involved—I was quite convinced it would have put everything at needless risk—I had discussed it with the newsdesk, and I also knew that the northern editor had kept his senior executive colleagues informed.

In any event, it was a wholly northern-based story and, during the five years I had been in Manchester, no instructions had been issued for the northern office to operate to the contrary. I was so angered by the unfairness of the reprimand that I offered to resign.

The editor called in a senior executive, who I guessed had played some part in my acutely uncomfortable position, and told him of my tendered resignation, which the editor had already declined to accept.

I returned to Manchester with the aim of getting off the newsdesk at the earliest opportunity. I knew by then that the incident had been engineered by certain executives in London to slap me down. I had blotted my copy book with the editor over the Crown Court case and, in particular, over the Press Council complaint, and I was vulnerable. It was an opportune time to strike.

The London office said that they would start the investigation all over again. But they never did. I have often wondered how many girls went through the dreadful trauma of an 'abortion' that was totally unnecessary, and were cheated out of a considerable sum of money.

I drifted through the next twelve months or so, which was marked by the retirement of the London editor. I did my best to appear enthusiastic but the commitment was no longer there. I no longer cared for the job, or the interests of the northern office. Above all, I had had enough of the executive world and its political games.

Chapter Six

The editor's successor was Nick Lloyd, a senior executive on the *Sunday Mirror*, who was later to become Sir Nicholas and editor of the *Daily Express*. He brought with him his wife, Eve Pollard, the *Sunday Mirror*'s women's page editor, and, from the *Daily Mirror*, sub-editor David Montgomery, a serious and unhappy Ulsterman who, several years later, following some political manoeuvring, was to be appointed chairman of the ailing Mirror Newspaper Group, publishers of the *Daily Mirror*, *Sunday Mirror*, *The People* and *Sporting Life*.

With the arrival of Nick and Eve came a radical change of editorial strategy to attract big budget advertisers targeting high-earning youngsters. It was a strategy that overnight signalled the end of *The People*'s traditional working-class identity and readership.

Staid and steady Mavis and her railway worker husband, Albert, living in their Sheffield semi, were yesterday's people. Now, in the Thatcher business boom philosophy, which created Essex Man, Tory-voting, two-car Sharon and Wayne, shacked up in Basildon and with cash to burn, were the target.

In flash, brash style, *The People* went all out for any kind of story which gave the inside dirt on show biz, the Royals—and soaps. It was the start of a tabloid soaps mania that made an earlier Bingo circulation battle between the tabloids seem quite rational.

The cause of *The People*'s particular sickness was widely credited to Eve—she was later to be appointed editor of the *Sunday Express*—whose reported logic was that as the soaps constantly topped viewer ratings charts, they clearly offered an untapped market of immense readership potential.

The People suddenly began to break new ground in TV soap sensationalism. Studios became awash with omnipresent 'insiders' and 'well-informed sources' who were crawling out of the woodwork, if not reporters' fevered imaginations, to reveal the latest soap-related scandal or twist in a soap plot.

Freelances with contacts on the studio floors, and who were able to pick up hot gossip on a TV soap actor's broken romance, unhappy marital state, sexual performance, gay/lesbian lover, drunken restaurant punch-up, or row with the producer, were the new elite. They were carrying cash away from newspaper offices in carrier bags.

Before long, every tabloid was on the soap train, and, so desperate was the competition, that fiction and fact began to get disarmingly blurred. Stories about the TV characters were written as if they were actually real people facing real-life dramas. Inevitably, it took tabloid skills to new levels of 'creative projection'.

I once received an anxious call from Eve, who expressed her concern that the Manchester office, a paranoid scream away from the Granada studios where it was produced, wasn't exactly covering itself in the glory of *Coronation Street* 'exclusives'.

She informed me that there were no family pets in *Coronation Street*. Why was that? Didn't the scriptwriters like pets? Let's have a story!

On another occasion, again the exasperation in her voice reflecting her disappointment, she pointed out that one particular controversial character in *Coronation Street* hadn't been in the Rover's Return for a couple of episodes. Were the scriptwriters planning a row? Let's have a story!

Every tabloid displayed a genius in its frantic and infantile efforts to outwit its rivals. The *Daily Mirror* was among the frontrunners with a truly desperate contribution: a centre-page artist's drawing of a dozen or so principal characters from *Coronation Street*, all of whom were in their dotage. The *Daily Mirror* had actually commissioned the artist to imagine how they would look in the year 2010 or thereabouts.

The effect on executives, alarmed at the thought of being caught out at editorial conferences about which soap star was doing what with whom and why, was quite startling. Senior executives, privately contemptuous of the new regime's editorial style, became extraordinarily knowledgeable of plots and casts.

One senior executive on *The People* played safe by having a video recorder installed in his office to record every episode of *Coronation Street*. The following morning, his first move was to catch up on the latest twist to prevent being caught on the hop by a call from Eve.

I confess, with not much shame, to letting the side down. Try as I might, I couldn't share the deadly seriousness of the editor and his wife in their keen pursuit of this garbage.

Nick had every right to expect a more positive

attitude from me, and some results, but I couldn't dredge up either. Whatever belief I had left in what I was doing, I still wanted to believe that newspapers had some purpose, even if it was tabloid-style investigations. At least, I reasoned, they were about real people.

His knowledge of soaps and the pop world was, to me, surprising. It was illustrated by an incident which occurred when we met by chance on our way into a city-centre hotel in Manchester where he had called a meeting of the northern executives.

At that moment, an unmade bed disguised as a long-haired teenage male came bounding past us and through the hotel's revolving doors. 'Do you know who that was?' asked Nick. I could only look at him dumbly and shake my head.

He was delighted to recognise a member of a leading pop group.

'He's their lead singer,' he explained. But I really couldn't have cared less if he had been the lead dancer with the Royal Ballet. I felt surprised that the editor of a national newspaper was able to recognise such a dimbo, or that it should give him such delight.

It reflected the difference between our news evaluation, confirming that I was on the wrong paper, and life continued to go downhill with every issue.

About twelve months after his appointment, I put a proposal to Nick, which I thought might make us both happy, at least for six months. I suggested I move my desk to Los Angeles for that period of time to file West Coast stories and features.

I had spent two successive holidays in Los Angeles, including a sabbatical. I had enjoyed the city's vibrancy and energy. I had also enjoyed the sight of news-stands groaning under the weight of publications covering every conceivable subject. It seemed a reporter's paradise.

Nick rejected my proposal, but agreed to a revised one, which would allow me to work unsalaried in Los Angeles for six months, filing material to *The People* on a freelance basis, but free to sell whatever might be rejected to other newspapers.

My wife Sue, and I agreed that if Los Angeles proved successful financially, she would bring out the family—in addition to Sam, seven, there was now Sophie, five, and Jessica, four—to a new life in the States.

A few short months after my meeting with Nick, I set up business in Los Angeles, in the kitchen of a cheap two-bedroomed apartment without air-conditioning, and which I shared with a battalion of kamikaze cockroaches, in an area of Hollywood Boulevard and Western reportedly known as Murder Mile.

The apartment was part of a spacious but old and neglected mock colonial-style house and adjoined the Hollywood Downtowner Motel in a locality which had probably been fashionable when Humphrey Bogart and Lauren Bacall were hot gossip items.

The furniture—a sadly sagging double bed, a desk-sized table and two chairs in the kitchen, and two battered armchairs facing a television set in the living room—looked as if it been thrown off a Buster Keaton studio set.

I stocked the fridge, had a phone installed in the kitchen, bought a pile of the latest newspapers and magazines, positioned my portable typewriter on the kitchen table, and the Los Angeles office was open for business.

During the next few weeks, I filed many 'offered

exclusive' story and features memos to the London office of *The People*. But from day one the response was deafening in its silence. It was puzzling and worrying. I knew that what I was submitting was tailor-made *People* material.

The follow-up phone calls I was putting through to the newsdesk were also being passed down the line to one of the messenger boys. Then it hit me. In making my plans for Los Angeles, I had overlooked one vital consideration: my relationship with certain executives in the London office. I really hadn't given that a second thought.

I had imagined that a good story would soon overcome any ill-will. But not so. I was not so much out in the cold as in the deep freeze.

In accordance with my arrangement with Nick Lloyd, I continued to file all story and features memos to *The People* first, and then to other tabloids, whose more positive response promised a lucrative future.

The day started at no later than 6am, due to the time zone difference, and rarely ended earlier than 8pm. It began and ended with the seemingly constant wail of police cars screaming along either Hollywood or Sunset Boulevard, the next block down, where straights and gays, and those in between, strutted their stuff in kinky leather, looking for business.

I lived off cheap TV dinners so full of chemicals that I was beginning to glow in the dark. The nights were invariably spent with The Lone Ranger and Tonto, before I fell asleep in one of the uncomfortable armchairs.

Worst of all, worse even than the SAS units of cockroaches which I feared might carry me off in the night, was the lack of air-conditioning. There was no release from a level of humidity which saturated my clothes within minutes.

To match the apartment, I bought a fourteen-year-old 'bargain' Toyota Corrolla wagon from the son-in-law mechanic of an exiled Scot I met in a bar. That didn't have air-conditioning either, but it did have lethal steering, a serious oil leak and very defective rear suspension which, with too much weight on the back seats or in the boot, caused the rear wheel arches to cut into the tyre walls. It looked a little out of place in Rodeo Drive.

Almost four months after arriving in Los Angeles, I received a letter from Nick Lloyd expressing concern at the lack of editorial direction in Manchester. If I intended to remain in Los Angeles, he needed to appoint a new northern news editor. He wanted to know what my plans were.

After six years as northern news editor I replied that I was happy to stand down. But, until Sue had had chance to view Los Angeles as a future home, I held back from resigning completely. It was agreed I would see out the six-month period and then decide.

Sue and the children arrived a couple of weeks later, by which time I had moved out of Hollywood and into a three-bedroomed apartment in a residential complex, complete with private swimming pool, tennis courts and gymnasium, in the nearby suburb of Anaheim.

We spent the next few weeks playing tourists in Los Angeles, San Diego and Mexico, spending the money I had earned. To the children, turning golden brown and living on a daily diet of ice cream and endless donuts, it was paradise. They were prepared to take out US citizenship the next day. Sue wasn't.

The more she saw of the laid-back, anything-goes LA lifestyle, the more concerned she became about its effect on our children. It was also clear that she would miss the different seasons, taking the dog for a walk, the Englishness of streets and shops, and a dozen other things which Los Angeles couldn't offer because it was, well . . . Los Angeles.

We spent many hours discussing the options. There weren't too many. Two months later, at the end of the six month period, we returned to England.

I sold the Toyota Corolla for a few dollars to a friend who was looking for something cheap for his son. As arranged, I left it parked for collection in a car park at LA Airport.

As the London-bound plane gained height, I looked out of the cabin window and saw it in the open car park area. I felt as if I was deserting an old friend.

Back in the UK, as a reporter once more, it was as if I had never been away. *The People* was pursuing as sensationally as ever a trashy mix of the best of the worst soap, show biz and speculative Royal trivia.

I did my best to avoid becoming involved by applying for a crime reporter's slot, which had just been vacated by a woman reporter who had no interest in the job. She had been appointed because it was thought she had the kind of figure that would encourage police contacts to confide in her.

It was a beat I would have enjoyed, and I expressed my keen interest to an executive whose support would have virtually ensured the appointment. I am still awaiting his response. Clearly, I was still out in the cold and on my way back to Manchester in the next available cattle truck.

My successor in the northern office was a former *Sun* reporter who had worked as a Saturday newsdesk casual and was to become editor of the *Sunday Mirror*. He gave me a warm welcome before I found a desk space in the newsroom.

I was never certain of the consensus of opinion to

my presence in the newsroom. It didn't really matter, although one reporter loudly observed for the amusement of one or two others: 'Oh, how are the mighty fallen!' The words stung for a moment, but that was all. Too much had happened for that kind of comment to penetrate too deeply.

Much more worrying was the effort required to adjust to the new-style paper. I tried, I really did. I made weekly trips to Leeds to call at the Yorkshire Television studios where the *Emmerdale* soap was being produced. I feigned interest as Rodney in the press office droned on about a particular actor or some new line in the plot.

I also tried to pick up any other show biz story, but it was a most painful, pointless business. I would drive away from the studio, without a story, feeling ashamed of myself. Not for failing to get a story, but for being there in the first place.

I even found it a teeth-gritting trial interviewing actors and actresses appearing in other Yorkshire TV productions, who, unlike most of the soap cast, at least had some claim to acting talent. I couldn't cope with them either.

Paying obsequious court to the precious luvvies seemed so unreal. The only positive consequence I saw of my trips to Yorkshire Television was that it helped to keep me out of the office—something that I was endeavouring to do more and more. It was preferable to sneaking glances at the office clock.

That I had become a clock-watcher, looking for any excuse to get me out of the office and end the day, underscored the lack of pride and satisfaction I felt in my work. I was doing no more than keeping my head down and picking up the money—an attitude I had once despised.

And yet at one time I had enjoyed the job so much that as a staff reporter in the London office, I volunteered to cover a job at Heathrow Airport on Christmas Day. I would work through the night and through the weekend without complaint in order to get a story. I would work on any kind of story with any kind of informant.

I believed in *The People* and I had respected the executives who wound me up and let me loose. Now I knew them, and there was nothing there; nothing to respect. I was in a vacuum, without the slightest idea of where I was going or what I wanted.

When I thought back on those earlier days, I could see how things had changed so much, or, perhaps, how much I had changed. It caused me to realise how trapped I had become. I couldn't go on with what I was doing, but I couldn't see what else I could do. I was a tabloid hack. That was all I could do. That was it. Full stop.

I tried to justify my salary by submitting memos to the newsdesk suggesting investigative features in which I might work. None was taken up, although one, while it got no further, raised some initial interest, sufficient to warrant a call on a couple featured in a local newspaper story on the Exclusive Brethren. That call was the first step on a journey that was to have a devastating effect on every area of my life.

The story told how the couple, David S. and his wife, had broken away from the extremist sect. They spoke in detail of the sect's harsh judgements on erring members, which had broken up a number of families, driven individuals to alcoholism and, in one case, suicide.

It suggested the kind of controversial feature that the *Daily Mail* had successfully run on the Moonies and the cult's brainwashing programme which had reportedly destroyed families and particularly emotionally susceptible individuals.

Coincidentally, the couple turned out to be near neighbours, living no more than a two-minute walk from my home. Their story was not an unfamiliar one: the parents of four children, they had been obedient members of the Exclusive Brethren all their lives, until they began to question the biblical basis of its stern and prohibitive rules.

They were made increasingly unhappy by the way in which friends, judged to have committed some slight misdemeanour contrary to the sect's Draconian code of religious conduct, were 'shut up' on the orders of the leading brothers.

It meant that they were denied any further association, socially, professionally or spiritually, with cult members, which included their own families. It was these divisions which had led to the break-up of families and even suicide.

The questions asked by David and his wife, as they probed the biblical basis of the cult's practices, caused the leading brother's judgement to fall upon them.

It was decided that David should be expelled, and an attempt was made to separate him from his wife by keeping her 'in fellowship', thus effectively breaking up their marriage.

It was a severely traumatic blow to the couple as, until that time, there had been no part of their lives since childhood that had not been spiritually or materially sustained by membership of the Exclusive Brethren.

The Brethren's decision caused David's and his wife's parents to disown them, and earnest attempts were made by the cult to seek, in the names of a Brethren couple, the legal adoption of their fourteen-year-old daughter. Such was the pressure and their distress that at one stage they came close to agreeing.

I spent perhaps an hour with David and his wife. I left touched by their gentleness, their lack of anger or bitterness, their courage, and the faith they still had in their God, despite what they had endured. I didn't expect to meet them again. They were Christians. I wasn't. We had nothing in common.

Some months later, though, I was to meet another Christian, a physiotherapist in a local hospital where I lay flat on my back in traction after a game of squash had aggravated an old slipped-disc injury. At the end of a week-long stay, she stood at my bedside instructing me on basic back-strengthening exercises.

She was very pleasant, kind and attentive. On the lapel of her uniform, she wore a small fish-shaped chrome badge. I asked what it represented and, after telling me she was a Christian, she went on to explain that Greek Christians, who had faced persecution and death following the crucifixion of Jesus Christ and the growth of Christianity, took the symbol as a secret sign of recognition. She had the same qualities of kindness and gentleness that I had noticed in my Christian neighbour and his wife.

I returned home inelegantly clad in a steel-ribbed corset, with instructions to rest in bed for a week. It offered a time for quiet reflection and thought. Thoughts came crowding in as I reviewed the life of this one-time messenger boy and I felt overwhelmed by unhappiness. Outwardly at least I had much to relish: a family I loved, an imposing five-bedroomed house, an executive-level salary, a company car and a lifestyle handsomely subsidised by company expenses which virtually paid the mortgage. How could I be dissatisfied? Yet I was. Deeply.

My family apart, none of it meant anything at all. I felt hopelessly discontented, without motive or purpose. The driving force of my life had been my job, and that force was certainly no longer there.

My work had been my identity, my security. Newspapers had created me, shaped me, and I had responded keenly and willingly. Now I no longer felt a part of newspapers. It seemed as traumatic and as emotionally haemorrhaging as a marriage break-up.

For some reason, I began to think about the gentle nature of the physiotherapist, which led to thoughts of David S. and his wife.

Some minutes later, on that Saturday morning, standing ramrod straight in my corset, I found myself on their front doorstep, asking: 'Can I come to church with you tomorrow?'

Chapter Seven

Trust in the Lord with all your heart
and lean not on your own understanding;
in all your ways acknowledge him,
and he will make your paths straight (Proverbs 3:5–6).

The church was light and modern in design, not at all like the daunting grime-covered Notre Dame cathedral that as a boy cub on special parade days I had attended because I wanted to carry the flag.

Instead of the intimidating interior architecture of endless arches, the chimney-stack organ pipes that reached the domed roof and a ritually ornate altar situated a short bus-ride away, there were rows of chairs separated by an aisle of carpet which led to a communion table, beyond which stood a plain lectern on a plain carpeted dais. At the back of the dais was a row of chairs and, either side, displays of flowers.

I followed my neighbour's cue in worshipping a God I hadn't spoken to since those nights at the side of my put-u-up bed when, as a sixteen-year-old, I was so keen to stay in journalism that I got down on my knees to beg a favour.

The service meant nothing to me. I had obviously

made a mistake. Before we parted company, my neighbour asked the question I was hoping he wouldn't: would I like to go to church with him and his wife the following Sunday? Out of politeness, I feigned a positive response.

The following Sunday we went through much the same style of worship and I experienced much the same lack of emotion. At the end of the service, my neighbour became involved in casual conversation with one or two of his friends. I stood by, staring at my shoes. I saw a piece of folded paper on the floor, no more than a few inches away. I picked it up and opened it. It contained a hand-written biblical reference— Proverbs 3:5–6—and nothing else.

I looked up the verses in one of the church Bibles stacked on a nearby table. It read: 'Trust in the Lord with all your heart and lean not on your own understanding; in all your ways acknowledge him, and he will make your paths straight.'

I put the piece of paper in an inside pocket and promptly forgot about it. But by the time I reached home, I had decided, without the need for an invitation, to return again to that church. It was the beginning of a new Sunday schedule, to which I looked forward with a strange enthusiasm.

My weekly church-going was starting to puzzle Sue, if not cause her some concern. Sunday mornings had previously been spent in bed reading the Sunday papers, followed by a late lunch and a busy time doing nothing.

Sue's concern was shared by my mum, then in her late seventies, who did her best to reassure Sue. I gather my mum couldn't make it out at all, but then it all became clear. 'Don't worry,' she told Sue, 'he's not going to church—he's going off on stories.'

I began reading the Bible daily. It was a mechanical exercise—a chapter a day—and none of it held any significance, particularly the Old Testament. I understood very little of what I read. I did it because . . . well, I wasn't sure. It just seemed the right thing to do. If I was going to church, it seemed to follow that I should read the Bible.

As the weeks passed, I should have tried to explain to Sue why I was going to church; the pleasure it gave me; the way I felt. But I didn't know how to start. Sue hadn't asked for any reasons, and I didn't proffer any.

But I now recognise that, however feebly, I should have attempted some kind of explanation. I can now imagine how threatened or isolated she might well have felt. That was the last thing I wanted. On the contrary, I wanted her to share what I had discovered. It was just that I didn't know how to raise the subject in a way that would make any sense in a house where church had long been dismissed as a weekly ritual for bigots and hypocrites. All the same, I should have tried to give her every reassurance.

I think she simply hoped that whatever was happening might quickly pass so that we could get on with our lives.

Certainly for my part, whatever was happening in my life, I had no difficulty in accepting it. There was no conscious awareness of the direction in which it was leading me. I simply wanted to know more of its peace and contentment.

I believe I was experiencing what St Augustine, the fifth-century theologian, described as God's 'prevenient grace', which gives life to the spiritually dead. It creates an inner dissatisfaction, inexplicable in human terms, to bring a person to a point of spiritual awakening.

Why someone like me was 'chosen' I cannot begin to understand, although I now know that God, contrary to the ways of this world, chooses the foolish to shame the wise (1 Corinthians 1:27). But then I had no understanding of God at all. He was a name, impersonal, unknown, which I couldn't bring into my frame of understanding. It was thoughts about Jesus that raised the questions.

As I understood it, this carpenter had a public life of three years, during which time he travelled around a very small part of the Middle East, reportedly performing some remarkable miracles and claiming to be the Son of God—a claim so heretical to the Jewish leaders of the day that they demanded, and achieved, his crucifixion.

But why such a fate? Why did his words and actions provoke such immense hostility that they should justify his execution? If he wasn't who he said he was, then surely he was either an imposter or, at worst, a highly schizophrenic religious extremist who would soon be forgotten.

His words and actions posed no real threat to the mighty and influential Jewish rulers. His words and actions were of love and peace, and even on the cross he asked his God to forgive his executioners.

All the same, I couldn't understand why countless numbers of people during the last twenty centuries had allowed themselves to endure all manner of sufferings, torture and even death for someone they hadn't met, spoken to or even seen, and who seemed so insignificant.

Yet all of history's kings and queens, politicians and military leaders, despots and dictators, radicals and revolutionaries, intellectuals and scientists, artisans and academics, have not equalled the profound and lasting impact this man, without political, military or financial might, has had upon the world.

Over the weeks that followed, I considered these questions that Jesus' life on earth raises. I simply accepted that Jesus had existed, what he had done and why he had done it. I could find no reason why I ought not to believe in him. And if I believed in him, then it followed, it seemed to me, that I should believe he was the Son of God.

The point about Jesus, I realised, is that he raises questions. I think it is impossible to consider him honestly without coming to a point where some disturbing self-questioning has to be faced. And that's the problem, for the answers can change people's lives. That's the threat he poses, so it is safer to dismiss him and those who follow him.

If my purpose in regularly going to church and reading the Bible was for no other reason than because it felt 'good', it was the only certainty in a life so directionless and meaningless and full of doubts.

And it was in this state, some weeks after I had knocked on my neighbour's door, that I stood up to sing the hymn 'Amazing Grace' in church one Sunday. I sang the words:

Amazing Grace! How sweet the sound,
That saved a wretch like me;
I once was lost, but now I'm found,
Was blind but now I see.

I felt so overwhelmed by those words that I couldn't continue singing. I could do no more than simply stand there, unable to hold back the tears that began to flow. I couldn't stop them. I couldn't account for them. It just happened.

With tears still running freely, I sat down, head bowed, and felt the hand of my neighbour, David, on my shoulder. I thanked Jesus for indeed saving someone like me. I found myself telling him how sorry I was for all the wrong things I had done during my life. I asked him to forgive my sins, and to come into my life. In that moment I committed my life to Christ.

I felt a little foolish at the way it had happened. It had been totally unplanned, at least on my part. I didn't hear any heavenly choirs or experience any sudden spiritual enlightenment.

But in the following days I came to experience a greater sense of well-being, a wholeness and 'cleanness'. I felt a security and joy that one might experience in suddenly realising that everything was all right. There was no sense of concern for the future; of unsettling anxiety. Everything seemed to 'fit', and I had a sense of purpose and wholeness.

But then during the weeks that followed that inner sense of quiet elation began to be overcome by certain doubts. Was I really good enough to be a Christian? Could Jesus really forgive someone like me?

In the way that I now know God spoke to me through the verse reference written on a piece of paper I found on the church floor (although I certainly didn't know it at the time), I know with no less certainty that he spoke to me to remove those doubts.

It happened as I sat in church, when my gaze fell upon an A4-sized Christian publication that had been placed against a leg of a chair in front of me. The text on the back cover was obscured but for the words in bold type: 'You are worthy.'

I knew in that instant, with absolute certainty, that God was speaking directly to me. As I would discover, he will communicate through whatever channel is necessary to give conformation or comfort in all circumstances or situations. At this time the certainty I felt, the conviction of the truth of those words on the back of that publication, came to me through the inner voice of the Holy Spirit.

Equally, in my spiritual frailty, I was unaware that the deep doubts I felt were the work of Satan, who will do all he possibly can to return to darkness those who turn to Jesus. The darker a person's former life, the greater his efforts to reclaim it. And he is persistent, as I found out time and again through my weakness.

God also spoke to me in two areas of my business life to both challenge and strengthen my commitment to Christ. On both occasions, he used speakers at my church. The first addressed the importance of young Christians at university making their commitment to Christ known as soon as possible. The longer it was left, the more difficult it would be, with the serious danger of them hiding their faith, if not denying it in the face of peer pressure.

I heard the message clearly. It made me concerned that unless in some way I publicly declared my commitment, particularly to my colleagues, I would quickly become a closet Christian. I wanted at all costs to avoid that danger. It would have been a denial of all I now claimed to believe. The problem, of course, was how best to do it.

Frankly, I wasn't looking forward to it. I knew that my commitment to Christ would make no sense whatever to my newsroom colleagues, hard-nosed cynics to a man. My credibility, or what was left of it, would be zero. It would be seen, I imagined, as the final disintegration of someone who had been quietly falling apart for some while.

I could hardly ask for their attention while I publicly

declared that I had become a Christian, or pin a statement on the notice board. Perhaps my best solution was to put a Jesus Christ sticker on the rear window of my car. It would be as effective as a prime-time TV ad. Tabloid reporters are nothing if not gossips. Once it had been seen, the news, no doubt to a chorus of incredulous laughter, would circulate with the speed of a bush fire.

While hardly an heroic gesture, I believe it was an important one. It not only told others where I stood, but also helped *me* to understand where I really stood, what really mattered in my life. I had publicly and professionally nailed my colours to Christ's cross. The public display of that car sticker increased my boldness in Christ.

Not long after this I experienced, most reluctantly indeed, a second nudging of the Holy Spirit. It came during a sermon which tackled the issues of honesty and ethics in business. Then came a most unwelcome voice from within: how could I possibly deny that my weekly expenses were anything but a blatantly dishonest fiddle? My heart sank.

The thought of losing each week a very considerable sum of money, which made a substantial contribution to the mortgage, filled me with despair. At every level in the newspaper industry, it was acknowledged that the right to submit phoney expenses was enshrined in the Magna Carta.

Any reporter, or executive, who submitted legitimate expenses would be considered unsuitable for his job on the grounds that he was clearly insane. I left church not at all happy about the decision I couldn't avoid, although I did try.

The following Tuesday, the beginning of a Sunday paper's working week, I sat at my desk with my completed expenses claim. It totalled, as I recall, about £110–120, which was my average unofficial weekly expenditure.

I felt the sharp prodding of the Holy Spirit, which I attempted to ignore by telling myself that everybody did it; that I needed the money; that losing so much money was going too far. But I found myself screwing up the expenses form and beginning again . . . and again . . . before the claim declared the genuine sum of about £40.

I felt no sense of virtue in what I had done—simply frustration and anger. Also, I felt afraid that I was travelling further down a road about which I was uncertain; further away from a world which gave me comfort and had kept me for so long in financial security.

It was difficult not to think that I was being a fool. Yet I realised that never again could I fiddle my expenses. My only comfort was the conviction that knowing Christ was more important.

I pushed myself even further adrift from my job by deciding to stop taking *The People* into my home. Among other things the page-three porn had become distasteful. The hypocrisy of that decision was not lost on me. I was willing to accept my salary from its profits, and enjoy all the benefits it gave, but I would not allow it in my home!

My hypocrisy was all the more stunning when it came to the job itself. There are a number of equally illuminating examples, but a story about a leading soap star's secret holiday romance with a pub barmaid makes the point.

It received major coverage by every popular national newspaper, and *The People*, like every Sunday tabloid, was keen to follow up with a sensational sequel. Predictably, the soap star's wife refused to be interviewed, but her mother, angered by her daughter's humiliation, was very willing to talk.

In an exclusive memo, I was supplied with her address and, a couple of hours later, I was sitting in her living room drinking coffee. She was in her late fifties, a still-attractive and stylish woman, who spoke well of her daughter, but unwisely of her unhappy marriage.

In her distress, I don't think she realised the hurt and embarrassment that her comments would cause in the cold light of sensational print. I did, of course. And I actively encouraged her.

I fully realised that as a Christian what I was doing was wrong, but as a tabloid hack, it was what I was programmed to do, and I wanted the kudos of the byline I knew the story would get. I eagerly included her every comment.

I also found myself prepared to resort to the usual rough-house tabloid tactics to protect my story. As I returned with the mother from her daughter's home, where she had tried unsuccessfully to persuade her to talk to me, a *Sunday Mirror* freelance hopped out of his car and hurriedly followed us along the driveway of her house in a desperate effort to talk to her.

Instinctively, I dragged him off the driveway and pushed him to the pavement from where he shouted threats of legal action for assault.

I finally drove away with an exclusive story safely in my notebook, which was to make a page three lead. As I anticipated, the story caused both mother and daughter some distress. What a farce my behaviour had made of my Christian commitment. But I didn't have the courage to resolve the issue by resigning. That wasn't even a consideration. I simply kept stumbling on, doing my best to satisfy the opposing forces in my life.

While I could discern no pattern then, I came to learn that God, in bringing us closer to him, takes us through any number of challenging and testing experiences, which are all part of his plan to strengthen and prepare us for the next stage of spiritual growth.

I came to understand much later that how we respond determines the progress of our spiritual growth. They are responses which he leaves us completely free to make, in situations in which he allows us to believe that we are in control. In that way, such is the marvellous mystery of his love, we answer with the truth of our hearts.

My next 'stage' took place over a period of eighteen months and involved three major investigations. I must say that I welcomed them. Anything rather than be involved in the paper's weekly schedule of show biz and soap drivel and dross, and I could still deceive myself into believing that their publication was in the public interest.

The first investigation named members of the aristocracy and the sons and daughters of leading City figures who were heavy users of heroin and cocaine and a variety of lesser drugs.

Over a three-month period, I worked with an informant, a former addict and supplier to the Sloane Square set, who, wired up with a miniature tape recorder, re-established contact and, by implying that he had a plentiful source, was able to obtain damning admissions of usage.

As a tabloid newspaper exercise, it was completely successful. For his efforts, the informant was paid a total of £9,000—£3,000 at a time in a three-part series—plus handsome expenses. It also doubtless caused a great deal of distress to parents and relatives, and indeed to the 'victims' themselves. In one instance,

I believe it led indirectly to the death of an addict, a young man in his early twenties, from a highly-respected family.

I remember him well because of a desperate and tearful plea made by his younger sister on his behalf when, with a photographer as a witness, I arrived at his Knightsbridge home on the Saturday morning before publication to give him the opportunity, as a legal caution, to comment on his confessed addiction.

In a state of sheer panic he phoned his sister, who, ten minutes later, sat by his side explaining that for some while her brother had been trying to end his addiction. He had recently got a job with a well-known company in the City, she added, and to be named in *The People* would finish him.

She pleaded with me to drop his name. I said there was nothing I could do. Everything was set for it to make the splash. She was still pleading as the photographer and I got up to leave the apartment. At the door, she screamed that I was a bastard. I replied that the bastards were the drug pushers. But she was right. I was just a different kind of bastard. We both lived off the likes of her brother.

The following day, the first part of the series appeared under the centre-spread headline: 'Lords of the Drugs Ring'. Everyone from the editor down was happy. But I wasn't. There was certainly none of the intense pleasure that the sight of such a spread would once have caused. I felt strangely flat.

About two years later, I learned by chance that that young man had died from an overdose. He had joined the Narcotics Anonymous and remained 'clean' for twelve months, but he had been tempted to take a small dose of heroin. It proved fatal. His system, no longer used to the abuse, couldn't cope with it.

I am not sure what part my story played in his death. But I am quite sure it did not help his survival. To his family, I can only say how sorry I am, and ask their forgiveness.

The second 'investigation' was into a Tory MP's sexual association with rent boys, invariably young, tragic runaway kids who prostitute themselves for a few pounds, or even just a warm bed for the night. The informant on this occasion was a gay pimp, himself a one-time rent boy, who had formed an 'agency' to provide teenage boys for gay sex.

In return for an initial sum of £80,000 to open a gay club in the north-east, a figure he later reduced to £20,000, he was willing to introduce me to at least one rent boy who would talk about his sexual involvement with the MP. That rent boy, it was planned, would agree to entice the MP to talk of their nights together in his West London flat.

Through the pimp's efforts, contact was indirectly made with a young homosexual who knew the MP well. Sickened by the sham of the MP's caring public image, he was prepared, without payment, to make a tape-recorded phone call to the MP's flat, followed by a night-time visit.

It all went according to plan, and the MP's disgrace was completed with the story of his downfall splashed across the front page in the most sensational tabloid style. The subsequent clamour of the media was to lead ultimately to the MP's resignation.

The pimp was not paid the sum he demanded. In fact, he was deliberately deceived by *The People*. Although I didn't agree with it, I knew he was going to be ripped off, and I was instrumental in that decision. I can vividly remember, with a drink in one hand and a cigarette in the other, sitting in a pub in Brixton with him and telling him about Jesus Christ and how he could change people's lives. He must have been impressed.

The third and final major story was another sex scandal involving rent boys, but this time allegedly with homosexual clergy. The informant was a sacked priest of doubtful sexuality who was seeking to embarrass the Church of England.

A nineteen-year-old boy was provided by the former priest and paid to make approaches to a number of clergy he claimed to be homosexual. It was probably the most pathetic and pitiful of the three stories.

Young and middle-aged ministers, including a senior churchman, were named in a front-page story and centre-spread feature. To maximise its impact, it was published to coincide with the beginning of the Church of England's General Synod.

During this time, while spending much of the week working out of the London office, I would return to my home in Cheshire to attend church every Sunday, continuing the hollow ritual of praying to God for his forgiveness for what I had done.

This eighteen-month period led to a crystallising of my thoughts. I began seriously to wonder whether I could operate at any level as a tabloid hack. The turmoil within was causing increasing despair. Nothing seemed clear.

I felt bad when I tried to do my best as a reporter, because I was clearly letting God down, and when I tried to act as a Christian in my job, I felt unable to function and respond in the way that I knew a reporter should. I was falling down on all fronts.

The direction of my future was brought into sharper focus by an invitation to return to the London office—an offer which, on my return from Los Angeles, I would have accepted with delight. It came from a senior executive shortly after the success of the third investigation. He asked me where I saw my future—in Manchester or in London? He asked if I'd like to return to the London office.

By then I knew that if I returned to London, it wouldn't be long before I was back in the trough, neck-high in the swill. Following those three stories, I knew how weak I had been, with thoughts of Christ far from my mind. I had found it too easy to put God to one side.

I knew it just wouldn't have been possible to continue as a Christian *and* produce the results London would certainly expect. I declined the invitation.

I have no doubt that the circumstances of my involvement in those investigations, their success and the invitation to London, were allowed by God for one reason: to put me in a position where I had to choose. In a sense, it was no choice at all, because God, in knowing me so well, knew the choice I would make.

But I couldn't know that then, as I understood so little of him. As far as I was aware, I was making the decision, and the one that I made cleared the way for God to take me further along the road with him, to a crossroads where the real walk with him would begin.

I would face that decision following three other stories, which also came in fairly rapid succession. The first two, even by *The People*'s standards, were notably sleazy. The third story, although no less so, had the added complication of a conflict of ethics involving a senior executive.

All this took place over some months and, as I had been doing for some time, I would drive off to a background of Christian music tapes and praying to God to keep me from doing and saying things which were wrong. It was a naïve and impossible prayer.

During his working day, the tabloid hack faces any number of situations in which he will say and do things inconsistent with even common morality or conduct, never mind God's ways. In a profession which is so manipulative and destructive, it cannot be otherwise.

The first story introduced me to that Glaswegian homosexual with whom I was briefed to spend the night in a gay brothel in order to witness orgies between adults and young boys.

In the second, I was briefed to find and interview the disciples of a satanist who had seduced teenage school-girls during graveyard rituals. He had been jailed at Leeds Crown Court after being found guilty of having unlawful sexual intercourse with two schoolgirls, which took place during devil-worshipping ceremonies.

My paper wanted to publish a graphic account of their activities, with particular emphasis on the sexual prowess of their sick and highly-disturbed leader, who, convinced of his control over women, had changed his name to Grigori Rasputin.

With information from a local freelance, it wasn't difficult to trace the squat home of a woman who knew Rasputin well. For a payment of £50, she will-ingly provided more than enough detail, factual and fictional.

She also helped me to trace a young couple who had rented a room to Rasputin in their semi-detached house on a housing estate. Astonishingly, they had made no objection when he erected a crude altar for devil-worshipping rituals which they could hear late at night, nor when he taught their young son satanic songs.

It wasn't until he pushed their son into a bush of nettles that they became concerned and told Rasputin to leave.

Rasputin had been so open about his satanic activities that when a local commercial photographer, trying to drum up business on the estate, knocked on the couple's door, Rasputin hired his services. The photographer took photographs of Rasputin stripped to the waist and daubed in satanic ritual symbols as, two-handed, he held a ceremonial dagger above his head, ready to thrust it downwards, before his home-made altar.

Through the photographer's calling card, a photographer and I called to negotiate the purchase of the negatives. For £1,000 he agreed to hand them over.

The following Sunday, my efforts made a page-three lead story, with the picture, cropped and enlarged to heighten the impact of Rasputin's dramatic pose, taking up most of the page.

My involvement with these stories continued to fill me with an increasing sense of despair at the way I was letting God down.

It was all so impossible, trying to please God and yet do my best in a world opposed to him. The two forces were pulling me apart.

Through all this, God was continuing to move things into place, preparing to put me in a position where I would have to decide, once and for all, whose camp I was in. About three years had passed since I committed my life to Christ, and everything that had happened since then had been in preparation for this moment.

The third and final story, in every sense, came through the London office. I was briefed to link up with a freelance in Cardiff who had information on a particularly brutal murder which had been running in the daily papers for several days.

A young pregnant mother whose car had broken down on a motorway was attacked while calling for assistance from an emergency services telephone. Police arrived to find she had disappeared. A few yards away was her car, with her young sister asleep on the back seat. Some days later the young mother's body was found.

A man was later charged with her murder. The freelance had traced his mistress to a once-thriving mining village near Cardiff. He said she had information to sell. My brief was to negotiate its purchase.

Within minutes of our meeting, the freelance explained that there was a problem. He said that a reporter and photographer from *The Sun* had also discovered the woman's address. The paper had promised to pay £12,000 for her exclusive story and picture.

But she trustingly spoke in detail of her relationship with the alleged murderer before signing a contract. When the reporter had heard enough, the photographer snatched her picture, and they made a rapid departure from her home.

It was now clear that she had little, if anything, to sell exclusively, and anyway, now that she had been conned, she was refusing to say anything. I phoned the London newsdesk to pass on the news to the senior executive who had put me onto the story.

He wanted a story, any story. He told me to promise her any amount of money to get her talking again. He didn't spell it out, but I knew what he was saying. Like *The Sun*, we would rip her off, but in fact more deviously.

Although *The Sun* had her exclusive story, the chances were that there would be something left which *The People* could bill as an exclusive, and, as she had spoken to *The Sun*, as we well knew, we would claim that she had broken our 'exclusive' contract to avoid fulfilling the financial terms of that contract.

I told the senior executive that I couldn't do it. For the first time in more than twenty years in newspapers, I was refusing a newsdesk instruction.

The executive replied that everyone was doing it and that we had to do it too. I remember his words clearly: 'It's the way things are these days.' He was right, but I still couldn't rip her off.

I left the phone-box unsure of what I was going to do, other than do my best to get a story without conning her. On my way back to her house I prayed to God to provide a way out.

Inside the small living room of her terraced house, I made no mention of any payment for her story. Instead, I explained that as she had told her story to *The Sun*, she no longer had anything to sell. I began to ask her casual questions about her former lover and, to my surprise, she responded.

As a routine question, I asked her if she had any photographs of them together. She said she had one or two, but had destroyed them when she heard what he had allegedly done. Then, as if struck by a sudden thought, she left the room for a few moments.

She returned with a colour photograph of her ex-lover, standing outside her home, barrel-chested in a Welsh Guards army uniform. It was enough to hang a tabloid story on. We discussed how much she would want for it. She agreed to an offer of £1,000.

A contract was despatched from London and the deal was signed. The photograph would be published some months later when her lover, who was found guilty of murder and sentenced to life imprisonment, finally stood trial.

I had obtained an exclusive picture story without the need to cheat the mistress. I returned to my hotel feeling unhappy about money being paid at all, but in trying to find some good in it all, I reasoned that at least the woman hadn't been cheated.

What struck me most of all, though, was what I had done in going against the instruction of a senior executive I had once much respected. I felt a finality about it, in the same way that I had put that Jesus Christ sticker on my car window, which, in effect, was a public statement challenging the rules of the paper I worked for.

By going against the senior executive on a major story, I had gone a good deal further, and I actually felt like a soldier who had refused to go into battle. In that decision, I believed I had put myself outside of newspapers; outside of the battlefield altogether. I was walking away from it all.

That Thursday night in my hotel bedroom, I made the decision to resign from *The People* on my return to Manchester. I felt very sad that my time on *The People* had come to an end. I remembered my freelancing days from the garden shed, getting a staff job, the first byline, and the ego-thrill of the many stories that followed.

But I also sensed, overwhelmingly, a feeling of freedom, of honesty and a rightness with God. I knew that what I was doing was right.

That night was frightening and seemingly endless. There were a dozen voices giving me every reason why I would be mad to resign: the consequences to my family, the confusion and concern it would cause Sue, the financial difficulties; the upset and confusion it would cause my mum who was so proud when I became a reporter; the laughing stock I would make of myself.

There was also a voice telling me that it would be

better if I were to end my life that night. I could do it by throwing myself out of the hotel window, it added. When people start to hear voices, especially urging suicide, it is considered time to get the straightjacket ready. But that's the way it was,

After a fitful night's sleep, the break of dawn finally came round, and my decision remained firm.

Chapter Eight

And we know that in all things God works for the good of those who love him, who have been called according to his purpose (Romans 8: 28).

I arranged to see the editor the following week to let him know of my decision to resign. I imagined it was probably not a decision he would attempt to dissuade me from.

I returned from Cardiff to receive a letter from him, which stated that while he had been told I was a good operator, he hadn't seen many results to prove it, and would I kindly get my finger out. It confirmed that the consequences of my problems with the job hadn't gone away.

The circumstances for the trip to London were good. A two-week family holiday had been booked in Cornwall, but I had forgotten to claim the period on the staff holiday rota. The first week clashed with another reporter's holiday.

It meant that Sue and the children would go to Cornwall as planned and I would join them for the second week. Normally it would have been a mild disaster, but not in these circumstances: it meant I would have the week alone to prepare myself for this meeting. It was a time when I needed to be alone.

As Sue spent the weekend happily preparing for the holiday, I didn't discuss my decision with her. I feared that if I talked it through with her, knowing the confusion and conflict she had already experienced through my Christian commitment, her probable reaction might cause me to change my mind. Indeed, I wasn't sure how I could even begin an explanation. It just wouldn't have made any sense.

However, the opportunity to tell Sue of my meeting with the editor came during a telephone call from her the following Tuesday evening. The call came as a surprise, and, equally surprising, I found I was able to tell her of my decision, quickly adding that I was confident I could meet our bills through freelancing, although not in the tabloid market.

I explained it all with some hesitation, still very unsure how she might react. The third surprise was her comment: she said she had faith in what I was doing; that she knew I would do what was best for the family.

As I waited for my appointment with the editor to arrive, I felt very much at peace. There was no anxiety or concern for the future. I knew with complete conviction that it was what God wanted me to do.

The sense of peace and calm I experienced was all the more remarkable given the way I had felt just four months earlier when the Mirror Group Newspaper publisher Robert Maxwell, following the introduction of computerised technology, authorised redundancy cuts which decimated the Manchester office.

We had sat at our desks, trying to appear relaxed and in control, like Death Row prisoners fighting against our emotions, as we waited to be called individually into the northern deputy editor's office to be told our fate. As reporters re-emerged their facial expressions told their story. Just three survived—a woman reporter, a photographer and me.

I felt very sad for those who found themselves out of work almost overnight. The redundancy notice was also brutally short, and a few, whose employment had begun many years earlier with Odhams Newspapers, would receive less than their entitlement due to a maximum pay-out figure arbitrarily imposed by Maxwell.

It was a miserable time of great change—a final proof that the carefree, high-rolling days of Mirror Group Newspapers were coming rapidly to an end. I praised God that I had been spared. I had felt inexpressibly grateful that I was still in work.

Yet now, just a few months later, I was quite happily preparing to hand in my resignation, without even the prospect of a redundancy payment. The fear and trepidation I had once felt at the thought of leaving *The People* had gone. Everything was absolutely right.

Having made the decision, the calm and peace, the quiet sureness I experienced during that week was amazing. It came through the power of the Holy Spirit. It was the grace of God creating within me a solid clearness of purpose.

On the Thursday morning, as I got ready for the train journey to London, that grace was expressed in another form. It came through my daily Bible study, *Every Day With Jesus* by Selwyn Hughes, which I had been reading for many months for its wisdom and encouragement.

The text for that day was from Genesis 15. The page lay open on my bedside table. In large bold type across the top of the page was a line from verse 1 in which God speaks to Abraham.

It declared: 'I am your shield, your very great

reward.' I knew that God was speaking to me. As he had spoken to Abram to comfort and reassure him in his circumstances, he was speaking to me in mine.

I sat relaxed in the editor's office, on a large leather-covered sofa unit, which extended around much of the room. The editor, John Blake, a former pop columnist with the *Daily Mirror* and a relatively recent appointment by Maxwell, came from behind his desk and sat on the sofa nearby.

He listened expressionless as I explained that I had become a committed Christian and that I couldn't go on working for *The People*, adding that I didn't feel I could achieve the kind of results he had a right to expect.

For a moment or two he didn't reply, unsure I think of what he had heard. Our conversation wasn't the kind that occurs too often in a tabloid newspaper editor's office. But I was surprised when he said he could understand my feelings, adding that in the circumstances he regretted sending me his letter.

This was followed by another, most welcome, surprise. 'How do you feel about redundancy?' he asked. As the Manchester redundancy quota had been achieved, it was not, I had thought, a live option. But it was fantastic news. It would make an enormous difference in helping to cushion the financial readjustments that would have to be made.

A few minutes later, he called the news editor into his office to tell him of our discussion. I had known the news editor for many years and he had known what sort of person I had been. As I explained to him about my commitment to Christ, I think he suddenly expected me to burst into laughter and admit it was all a bizarre send-up. He looked, to put it mildly, a little mystified. He said very little.

John Blake then called in the editorial director. I had known him too, from the day I had joined *The People* fourteen years earlier. On hearing the news, he said nothing, just stared at me, convinced no doubt that I was badly cracking up. He was told by the editor to make the necessary redundancy arrangements.

Afte shaking hands all round, I walked out into *The People* newsroom for the last time. Reporters who had seen me leave the editor's office were, as ever, curious to know what was going on. 'Are you coming back to London?' shouted one. I smiled and shook my head.

The newsroom seemed such an alien place. I had once been excited by just sitting in a newsroom, any newsroom, keen to get away on another story. Now there was nothing, no emotion at all. The place where I used to get a buzz from simply sitting in, now meant nothing to me. I was a stranger.

I walked out of the Mirror Group Newspapers building in Holborn and towards Chancery Lane to catch a tube. At the tube station steps, I stopped briefly to look at a statue of a soldier erected to honour the fallen dead of the first world war.

My memory flashed back many years to a time when, as a fifteen-year-old messenger boy, I had passed that statue daily on my way to work at the nearby offices of Associated Press in Farringdon Road. I remembered cracking a joke about the soldier's bayonet to another messenger boy and he fell about laughing. It was an incident that had occurred twenty-eight years earlier, in another life.

Within a week of my resignation, I received a phone call from a freelance who was a correspondent of the *UK Press Gazette*, the journalist's trade magazine. He had at one time worked as a freelance for *The People* and he apparently couldn't reconcile the reason behind my decision and the character of the person who had made it.

It would, he added, make a good story for the *UK Press Gazette* and proposed an interview. I gave it a moment's thought and agreed. It wasn't a proposal that required much thought. I had made a practice of talking about my commitment to Christ at any time to anyone. I felt that if I started backing off, I would soon end up in the closet, too frightened to admit openly what Jesus had done in my life. It would be a betrayal of God and make a nonsense of what I had done.

I realised that there would be reporters who would read the news with scorn and scepticism. One former colleague cynically joked that I had become a Christian to get the story on the kidnap of Terry Waite, the Archbishop of Canterbury's envoy, who at that time was being held hostage in Beirut. Another, actually an executive on a religious newspaper, asked me whether I had claimed to become a Christian as a ruse to get redundancy.

Some days later, a full-page feature appeared in the *UK Press Gazette* in predictable 'tabloid hack finds God' style. It was illustrated with anecdotes of the ways in which, as northern news editor, I had callously exploited people and situations.

In responding to the freelance's questions about the lies and deceit of gutter press newspapers, I spoke more critically of *The People* than perhaps was politically wise, particularly as I had yet to receive my redundancy payment. On the morning of the feature's publication, I received a phone call from a senior executive on *The People*.

He was most unhappy about the comments, which,

he added, had put my redundancy in considerable danger. At that moment, he said, the editor was in Maxwell's office, trying to cool him down. None of it, I later discovered was true. But if that executive had hoped to cause me some sleepness nights, he succeeded.

Sleepness nights were something I would need to get used to. They began soon after I realised that I wouldn't be able to freelance after all, despite my reassurances to Sue. I had done so successfully from a garden shed sixteen years earlier, and even from a kitchen in downtown Hollywood five years earlier, but I was dealing with the tabloid market, which I knew so well.

Now I intended to concentrate on features for so-called quality magazines. That was the plan, but I was quickly to discover that it wouldn't be that easy. It was a market in which I had no contacts whatsoever; I had optimistically believed that doors would soon open with the right kind of features ideas.

But the style of the magazine world is very different from that of the tabloids, and, frankly, the plummy-voiced Fionas and the luvvie Tristrams was a double-act I knew I wouldn't be able to live with. I knew their phoniness too well to believe it or trust it. I would have been swapping one kind of media garbage for another.

Similarly, I didn't have the all-important contacts to establish a market with the quality newspaper magazines, and nor was I likely to find them. A forty-three-year-old former gutter press reporter based in Manchester, who had resigned from his newspaper because he had become a Christian, was a suspicious character who was not going to receive any red-carpet welcomes.

Besides, due to the number of newspaper redundancies taking place, the market was not short of good writing talent—much of it on a more skilful level than mine. As the inevitable conclusion dawned that I was going to have a tough time earning a crust as a free-lance, the nights became longer and darker.

The mocking voices returned to tell me how I had screwed up; how I was making an idiot of myself, and how I would soon be in deep financial trouble, with all the distress that would cause my family.

I would suddenly awake every morning at 4am, almost to the minute, with my heart pumping loudly, as if it were about to burst out of my chest. There would be a very real sense of fear gripping the pit of my stomach, and my forehead would be heavy with a peculiar, prickling sweat.

In this state, I would lay in bed, my eyes tightly closed, trying to fight the voices by reciting over and over again the only biblical passage I knew by heart—Proverbs 3:5–6, the reference I had found written on that piece of paper on the church floor, which told me to trust in the Lord with all my heart—and the Lord's Prayer.

I had no depth of faith, and very little understanding or knowledge of God's word and its ability to protect in battles of spiritual warfare, which was what those nights were about. In my spiritual immaturity, I was vulnerable to a lifetime's fears. I had nowhere to run, no refuge in which to hide. I had to begin to learn to trust in the Lord.

Once again, I also heard the voice that told me to end my life—not by throwing myself out of a window, as in the Cardiff hotel, but by hanging myself in the garage.

They were nights that cannot, I think, be understood unless endured. All I could do was cry out in my mind for Jesus Christ. But none of it, no matter how hard I prayed, seemed to make any difference.

The peace and contentment I had experienced were far from me now. There was no sense of security, no certainty that everything was all right. Just total fear and despair.

It was a fear that was so real that I began to dread going to bed. After several days, I welcomed the exhaustion because it usually meant a sound night's sleep, but then, refreshed, the cycle would start all over again.

I would sometimes lie in the dark going over what I had done and why I had done it, questioning the motive, and whether I really had to resign from *The People*. The answer came back to the same point: I had had no choice.

Could I have fixed up another job in the media? I didn't think so. Tabloid or so-called quality newspaper—its's the same deception. It simply comes in different disguises to suit the market. That's why, when it came down to it, I couldn't put my heart into freelancing.

These were thoughts and feelings I couldn't tell Sue about; they would have made no sense to her. It was enough that I felt such dread and confusion about everything. To have caused her similar alarm would have helped neither of us.

Many months later I was to read of Martin Luther's words, when, in defending justification by faith which led to his ex-communication, he said: 'Here I stand. I cannot do otherwise, so help me God.'

Forgive the comparison, but that is exactly—*exactly*—how I saw it. What I had done I had done because I couldn't do otherwise. If there had been an alternative, an easy option, I would gladly have seized it. But there was no compromise. The choice was either to go on with Christ, or reject him. And that was no choice.

About three months after my resignation, in a state of tiredness, confusion and anxiety, I rationalised a trip to London, without God, to speak to one or two former colleagues whom I had known in Manchester. They were now executives on middle-market tabloids, not the gutter press end. Freelancing for them, I assured myself, would be all right.

I went desperately looking for some hope, some encouragement. I wanted to return with something positive to tell Sue. But it didn't work out. It was simply embarassing all round. By early evening, with the rain sheeting down, I walked along Fleet Street, past newspaper offices I had once hurried through as a messenger boy in days which had been so easy and uncomplicated. I had about £1.50 in my pocket and a good deal less in the bank.

As I passed a phone-box, I impulsively decided to call a national newspaper editor I knew quite well, to see if I could call in the next day. I proposed to ask him for a staff job, regardless of its effect on my commitment to Christ.

I was so wracked with worry that I didn't care what others—former colleagues or Christian friends—might think. I really felt I couldn't go on this way. I had to ease the financial pressures.

I was midway through dialling the newspaper's number when I stopped, unable to complete it. I just stood there holding the phone, realising what I was doing. I was turning my back on God, running back to all the things that had been destroying me. All that had happened in the last three years, and the joy I had known in knowing God, would have been thrown away. I suddenly realised how far from God I had been that day.

I left the phone-box to catch a tube to Euston Station for the return journey to Manchester. It had been a bad day indeed. I knew then for sure that it would be impossible either to freelance, or even to consider a staff job. My days in the media were truly over.

I wasn't looking forward to breaking the news to Sue, who had expressed so much faith in me when I confidently told her that I could once again establish a profitable freelance business.

That night I was awoken following a dream which perhaps will make sense only to those who have been on this journey. The dream was of a raging, whirling, turmoil of colour and noise. It was as if I was looking on at whatever was happening. Then I heard the clear message that the media was my Egypt and I was not to return.

I awoke with those words so clear in my mind. This time there was no sense of fear, no pounding heart or sickening feeling in my stomach, no prickly sweating brow. Instead a sense of peace and great calm returned to me.

I knew by then enough of my Bible to understand the meaning of the message. In answer to their pleas, God had rescued the Israelites from the bondage and slavery of Egypt to establish a new home in the promised land of Canaan. But, overcome by their fears and anxieties, they soon began to complain bitterly of the hardship of their travels. They longed to return to Egypt, ready to accept even slavery in return for a plentiful source of food and drink.

In the same way, alarmed by the sudden hardship of my new circumstances, I had been looking back to the media, to a job which kept me in highly-paid bondage to my fears and insecurities. And as the Israelites, through their lack of faith, were constantly to disobey

God as he guided them to the land of milk and honey, so would I be tempted to rebel as he led me through my spiritual wilderness.

My disobedience, caused by such little faith, would bring me down time and again, until, completely broken, I would finaly come to understand that I could do nothing in my own strength; that I could survive only through the power of his grace. Understanding and knowing the power of this truth was a long way in the future, however.

As I look back, with all the sureness of 20/20 hindsight, I find it remarkable how God created the circumstances of the 'wilderness' through which I would need to travel, in order to begin to understand something of the mystery of his ways. I can see the wisdom and rightness of his actions in all that has happened. I can see how he has unfailingly provided just enough to meet the needs of the moment. It was this way following my resignation, at the time of my disastrous freelancing efforts.

I was invited to edit a forty-four page Christian booktrade magazine, which meant writing virtually all the stories and features, including the headlines. It paid £500 a month and covered no more than a mortgage reduced by the redundancy payment, and the milk bill.

Although it was sufficient to prevent a major financial haemorrhage, it was far from enough to stop the bleeding altogether. It put a brake on the slow slide into increasing debt. And I can see now that it was a necessary part of God's plan for my life at that time. It prevented the sense of financial security that had fed my proud and arrogant self-sufficiency for so long.

If on resigning from *The People*, I had walked into a job offering a similar salary, I would have learned nothing of Christ. Instead, I would have congratulated myself on the success of my changed circumstances, smug and self-righteous in my new-found security.

The fact is I had to learn how to live in the strength of Jesus Christ, which could only happen by God first exhausting me to the point of complete helplessness and hopelessness, and the first stage was to remove financial dependence upon myself.

There was also another aspect to this situation: it helped me to become more sensitive to the hardships of others. I began to see people through new eyes and I was able to feel their pain and sadnesses. It also helped me to see the reality of the family of Christian brothers and sisters. It was a lesson which caused me so much hurt and bewilderment.

Apart from David S. and his wife, who were always there with their prayers and friendship, I received from my brothers and sisters in Christ no gesture of guidance or understanding, no reassuring words, or invitation to spend time in their company, or in prayer.

Instead, as I stumbled and staggered in my milk-and-water spiritual frailty, I saw Christians who were so successful in their businesses and so happy in their marriages and who seemed so secure and stable in their faith and Sunday companionship of each other that they seemed miles away from me and what I was experiencing.

I didn't know them and they didn't know me. We were so distant from each other and I couldn't understand why. It wasn't the way I though it would be. Where was this Christian brotherly love?

The attitude of one Christian, who would stand in church eloquently praising the Lord for his love and compassion, left me devastated at a time when I was experiencing considerable guilt for the problems and unhappiness I was causing my family.

Over a cup of coffee, following a church service, he asked how things were going, and I replied, 'Not too well.'

'Well,' he asked, 'did you really have to resign? Couldn't you have got a transfer to another department?'

His tone implied that I had gone too far in resigning; that it probably hadn't been necessary. I was too confused by his questions, and too unsure within myself and too tired physically, to find the words to explain or defend what I had done. He either didn't understand what a tabloid hack has to do, or he didn't understand Christ.

At a particular time when I would have broken down in gratitude for an encouraging smile, his questions cut into me deeply, and loaded greater guilt on me. I left church feeling even more isolated, in a state of sorrow and confusion that seemed to have become a way of life.

I also felt rejected by the words of a vicar—an elderly and academic man whose church I had attended on several occasions because of the encouragement I received from his sermons. I believed that he would understand what was happening in my life and that he could tell me how I could be stronger in my faith.

In utter desperation, I phoned him one morning to explain that I needed to talk to him. I explained about the nights of sleeplessness, the chaos all around me, and that I would appreciate the chance to talk to him.

I referred to spiritual warfare, a subject which unsettles many Christians. They prefer not to think of Satan because such thoughts frighten them. It quickly became clear that it was a subject this vicar preferred not to discuss.

He failed to respond to my request to call on him. Instead, he advised me to stop thinking about Satan, buy a bottle of brandy and have a glass before going to bed. Confirmation of my fragile state was the fact that I actually followed his advice and bought a half-bottle of brandy I couldn't afford. It did nothing to help.

Away from my church, I met others like me: men and women, egg-shell weak, who were going through their own battles. I saw the rebuffs they endured within the Christian family, and I could make no sense of it.

I saw a timid and nervous woman, struggling to recover from the terrible suicide of her husband, brought to tears by the harsh words of her Christian employer. He was a man who knew God's laws so well, but who knew little of the love of Jesus Christ.

I looked on as one brother, a middle-aged man who, like me, had come late to Christ, and who had suffered a great deal of tragedy, broke down in tears because of one humiliating rebuke too many from a fellow Christian.

I tried to calm down a young man in his early twenties, a former drug addict and supplier, who was growing daily in his love of Christ, but who wanted physically to strike out in anger at the constant provocations of another Christian.

What I saw and experienced of the Christian family in those days most certainly intensified my fears. I couldn't reconcile what I was experiencing with the teachings of Christian unity and fellowship. Before my resignation, during the many months I had attended church weekly, my perspective had been unchallenged. It hadn't been tested. Now it very much was.

It was as if the rug had been pulled from under my feet. At night, when the fears were particularly strong, a negative voice would tell me that at least I had known where I stood in tabloid newspapers, even in the gutter press. I knew that the first and last rule was to look after number one and get results. It was as uncomplicated as that. In that sense there were no double standards. I had known precisely where I stood. But now, among Christians, I was certainly not so sure. When I heard, much later that it is unwise to judge Christ by the standards of Christians, I understood why.

But there was comfort in this, because it caused me to realise that no Christian could have brought me to God: only his power could do that.

I couldn't understand at this time what was going on—why God was putting me through this experience—but I can now see that I had to learn to depend only on him, not on myself, or the local vicar, or the Christian family. My strength was in Jesus Christ. That was what he was working to show me.

It was all part of the necessary process to create the circumstances in which I could be challenged and tested, just as Job was. In reply to his critics Job said in chapter 23, verse 10: 'But he knows the way that I take; when he has tested me, I shall come forth as gold.'

I also believe that God put me in those circumstances so that I might learn the importance of love and compassion for other Christians. Due to all sorts of crises and deeply-buried wounds, weaknesses and insecurities, many hang on daily to the cliff-edge. For Christians to stamp on their fingers, through indifference or harsh biblical legalism, grieves God beyond words.

It is so easy to be like the Pharisees who believed that money and success could be equated with godliness; who believed that ritualistically following God's laws was all that mattered. Misfortune or tragedy was caused, they reasoned, by unrepented sin. It gave them a hardness of heart which allowed them to walk by as a brother lay dying.

It can be so easy for those who are blessed with relatively untroubled and peaceful lives, to uncaringly dismiss another Christian's difficulties as being due to nothing more than lack of faith. 'If only you had faith,' we crow, 'your troubles would be over.'

If we know little of testing or turmoil, we cannot begin to understand the spiritual desperation of those who struggle on, longing for just a fraction of the strength of Christ in order to survive the day.

How easy it is to recoil at the sins of those who exist beyond our social boundaries—people we reject because they don't quite fit the Christian stereotype. We can forgive the white-collar fraudster, the adulterous lawyer or the wife-beating executive, and so we should, but we cannot embrace the drug addict, the prostitute, the homosexual or the down-and-out.

If you are new to Christ, beware of those attitudes and pray for those who demonstrate them. Ask the Holy Spirit to guide you to Christians who stand and work in his power. If you seek to know more of Christ, you will recognise them.

I want to balance my bad experiences of the Christian family by praising God for the many Christian brothers and sisters who, when the time was right, encouraged me. It is impossible to express my gratitude for their support, patience and prayers; for their compassion and kindness, their willingness simply to be there whenever I needed the strength of their company. How I praise God for them.

If you are a person new in Christ, and for all sorts of

reasons possibly going through a great deal of hurt and confusion, I would stress that whatever your circumstances, if you desire to know more of Christ, you are there because it is where God wants you *for now*.

In our stumblings and failings, our relationship with God through the Holy Spirit brings us to greater freedom and growing understanding of him and his power.

Our enemy, the Father of Lies, does not give up easily. The darker your past, the more he will fight to retain his control, to return you to darkness. He will use any tactic and anyone, from friends and family to Christians, to achieve that end.

At these times, we must turn to Christ, talk to him of our fears and despair; seek his guidance and his strength through his word—particularly when it is the last thing we want to do—and through it we come to the peace and contentment of the Holy Spirit which strengthens in all circumstances. In this way, we begin to learn to endure every situation and circumstance in his strength.

With freelancing no longer an option, I made determined attempts to interest a number of companies in house newspapers. I came close to succeeding a couple of times, but I didn't have the back-up capital, nor the shop window razzmatazz, and nor, by now, the necessary confidence to make it work.

I would pray for days before making presentations at meetings at which I would arrive dog-tired and dispirited. I had, I am sure, the look and smell of failure. Some days were worse than others, and there were moments when my life seemed unreal, as if it were all a bizarre dream.

This was particularly so on days when, to save the

price of a bus ticket, I would walk from the railway station and across Manchester city centre to the office where I edited the Christian book trade magazine.

It was a route that would take me past hotels and restaurants, through the city's Chinatown, where I had once drunk and dined with no thought of bills met by expenses. There was one restaurant, a small exclusive Italian place down a flight of stairs, where a million years ago I had eaten with senior executives. It had been a night of sharp suits, an open menu and plenty of wine.

Those days could not have been in sharper contrast to a working day in which lunch was now bought in a nearby sandwich bar where I would collect a takeaway cup of soup and a sandwich. The decision as to which kind of relish to have was actually a high spot of the day.

The surreality of it all struck me, for a different reason and in different circumstances, late one night as I stood on a near-deserted platform at Manchester's Piccadilly Station waiting for a train home. It had been a particularly bad and depressing day when I met by chance a successful Christian businessman. I looked down and felt down.

He was on his way to London, in a sleeper, he explained, to negotiate a major contract. I stood there, with little to say, trying to smile confidently, hoping he wouldn't ask how I was doing. He didn't.

As he continued to tell me how incredibly well he was doing, I felt good for a few moments, just being part of his positive dialogue. Then suddenly he was gone, with purple mohair scarf trailing in his slipstream.

As I mumbled goodbye, it struck me that on the evidence of his clothes, manner and style, my Christian

brother could have been a newspaper executive interested in nothing beyond his own world. In those days
there was so much that seemed upside-down—so little
I understood.

At about that time, while in conversation with two
Christians, one, who had also worked for Mirror
Group Newspapers, remarked to the other for reasons
I can't now recall that he couldn't have resigned—he
didn't, he said, have my strength of faith.

If he had only known how many times I had broken
down in despair and would continue to do so, wracked
by fears and anxiety out of control, he would have
known how little faith I had.

Chapter Nine

My son, do not despise the Lord's discipline and do not
resent his rebuke, because the Lord disciplines those
he loves, as a father the son he delights in (Proverbs
3:11–12).

God's timing, in reassuring us of his presence in anxious and anguished times, is impeccable. His reassurance comes to encourage, to give hope, and sometimes
to resolve a problem, and always at the right time.

I would experience this frequently through a variety
of sources: a verse, or even a line, from the Bible, a
hymn, Christian music, a sermon, or through a passage
received from other Christians, or in more unusual circumstances.

An example came in a phone call after a long night
in which I had allowed my fears once again to run riot.
I had fallen asleep some time after dawn, and the
phone on my bedside table startled me into conscious-
ness.

I grabbed the phone, looked at the bedside clock—it
was precisely 9.27am—and tried to make sense of the
voice booming down the phone. 'Listen, brother,' said
an exuberant voice, 'the Lord has told me to call you to

let you know that there are hundreds of men up here in Scotland praying for you!'

The voice belonged to a Scotsman called Drew Greenwood, who was then President of the Glasgow chapter of the Full Gospel Business Mens' Fellowship International. He had read, or heard about, the feature in the *UK Press Gazette*, and had somehow managed to obtain my ex-directory phone number.

The love and encouragement of his words came at a time when they were never more needed. Believe me, they gave me the strength to get through that day, and also left me with something to look forward to. Our conversation ended with an invitation from Drew to be his guest at an FGBMFI weekend rally in Scotland, where literally hundreds of Scotsmen were meeting to worship God.

A few weeks later, I received a phone call from a Christian businessman, based in Wakefield, Yorkshire, who had also traced my phone number. He travelled to Manchester to spend some time in conversation. On his way over, he said the Lord had clearly given him a word of encouragement for me from Isaiah 62:3–5.

They were encouraging words indeed, but in my condition I found it very difficult to believe that I could ever be 'a crown of splendour in the Lord's hand, a royal diadem in the hand of your God'. In fact, I wasn't sure what it meant.

I was also to meet in the months ahead another Christian businessman, a consultant to a major property company. Most times we met when he was visiting Manchester, over no more than a cup of tea in a local hotel. This man, more than most, knew of my difficulties, but not of my fears, and when we parted a familiar sense of fearful isolation would return.

But these were men who were strong in Christ and

their strength strengthened me. I felt secure in the presence of their faith. It was in these ways that God was constantly with me to hold me up.

A further, more dramatic, example of God's timing came in the arrival, just one month and two days after my resignation, of Elizabeth, our fourth child.

She had not been planned—at least not by Sue and me. But I have no doubt at all that she was an important event in God's plans for Sue. I believe Liz's arrival helped Sue, a very maternal woman, to quell her concerns and worries about the family's circumstances. She was able to lose her fears in her love for Liz. I think in those most difficult days Liz gave Sue a much-needed diversion from all that was happening around her.

Certainly there seemed to be little I could do to reassure her that things would work out. My efforts to talk to her about how I felt, or my belief that God would bring us through it all, seemed futile, because there was now so much uncertainty within me.

Sue had a husband who was clearly going through some bizarre crisis which was turning her world upside-down, if not threatening to destroy it. The serious problem was that I was no longer the man she had married.

What had once been meat and drink to me—image, ambition, success, material acquisitions—were now meaningless. The people I had once admired—the sharp operator, the neat-suited wheeler-dealer, the so-called movers and shakers—were as nothing; merely insignificant men seeking substance in their shadows.

And what I had once scornfully dismissed—Christianity and its dull, wimpish and hypocritical followers, and all they represented—I now enthusiastically embraced, because I had came to understand the incredible love, strength and courage of Jesus Christ, and I wanted to know much more of him.

The cause of Sue's concerns lay all around, in bills that couldn't be paid, in nights out that could no longer be enjoyed, in clothes that couldn't be bought, in holidays that couldn't be taken.

The best I could do was to apologise for what I was putting her through, but that gave little consolation. This increased my sense of guilt and failure, and all I could do was to keep praying to God to help us. I know those days tested Sue's loyalty to the limit.

To help ease the financial pressures, Sue, now that she was at home with Liz, became a registered child minder. Suddenly there were children swarming all over the house, but, despite all the pressures, she continued to cope.

It was tough on the children too, with even their pocket-money coming to an end. It prompted Sophie and Jessica, then aged ten and eleven, to go out with a bucket and sponge to wash neighbours' cars. And when my son, Sam, then thirteen, wanted a mountain bike, he worked two newspaper rounds until he raised the money.

I felt sad and helpless, but above all I felt very proud of them. It caused me to reflect, yet again, on the consequences to my family of my commitment to Christ. My sole comfort was that I knew Christ understood and that he was with us and would not allow my family to be harmed.

In providing the consultancy editorship of the Christian book trade magazine, God was not only supplying the money to at least cover the mortgage, but he was also giving me encouragement through people whose lives he had amazingly transformed.

One of the most remarkable testimonies was that of a former prostitute, who many years earlier lost custody of her baby son after the local social services claimed her to be an unfit mother.

She became a heroin addict, and to finance her addiction she turned to prostitution. She was slowly destroying herself. At that point in her life, when it was as its very lowest, she met a Christian woman whose love and concern caused her to invite Jesus Christ into her life.

She described to me the remarkable changes that followed. She was able to finish with her life on the streets, her addiction to drugs, and was able to get a regular job. She also began praying to be reunited with her son, by then a young man aged about seventeen.

In circumstances which I can't accurately recall, a reunion actually came about and he moved into the home his mother had now established. And it led to him too making a commitment to Jesus Christ.

Shortly before they were to take part in a church-sponsored charity walk, and about three years after they were reunited, the son was tragically killed in an industrial accident. The woman knew that the walk, on Mothering Sunday, was something her son would have wanted her to take part in. In his memory, accompanied by other Christians, she did so.

During that walk, on a quiet stretch of countryside road, a single-decker bus passed slowly by. Looking out of the rear window of the bus, she saw the face of her son smiling at her. He was also recognised, she said, by another Christian walking by her side.

The bus disappeared round a bend further down the road. As the walkers turned that bend, a bouquet of cellophane-wrapped flowers was lying in the middle of the road. They were the woman's favourite flowers, and the kind that her son had bought her each Mothering Sunday since their reunion.

As she told me the story over the phone, we ended up choking back the tears together. To non-Christians, and perhaps even to some Christians who haven't experienced the power of God, it is probably a story too fantastic to be credible—simply the mystical imaginings of an emotionally distraught woman. But I knew the miracle he had performed in my life. To me, it was easy to believe.

At the time of the interview, this woman was working to raise the capital to open a residential hostel for prostitutes and drug addicts in need of support and guidance.

I also interviewed a man who, fired by his company as head of their North American operations, returned to the UK without a job and under great financial strain. He had a large family, was used to a very comfortable lifestyle, and now had a capital worth of no more than £6,000.

In utter desperation, he fell to his knees and prayed to God at 3am one morning, pleading for any kind of job. A day or two later, he had a meeting to raise venture capital to launch a business.

The meeting was successful and led to the opening of a shop which was the beginning of a multi-million-pound high street retail chain. He became heavily involved in church work, was generous in helping others, and is a tremendous witness to the power of Jesus Christ.

The magazine also brought me into contact with an American businessman called Jack Eckerd, who became a friend of Charles Colson, the senior aide to President Nixon who was jailed for his part in the Watergate scandal.

Before becoming a Christian, Jack owned a chain of

1,700 drugstores in fifteen states, with an annual turnover of $2.5bn. He had run for state governor and the US Senate, with social and business contacts in political circles all the way to the White House. But whatever he had, it wasn't what he was looking for.

Through meeting Colson, he eventually became a Christian, which led to him selling his drugstore empire. With his business acumen and organisational skills, he set up a foundation to operate camps in five states to help problem juveniles.

He also headed up an agency in Florida to run the state's prison industries, which brought him into contact with prisoners, some of whom, through his personal testimony, came to Christ. Jack said: 'Jesus has put my life in perspective. Nothing else and no one else could have done that. . . I have a deep peace that I never had before. That empty feeling has left.'

It is worth noting that Jack finally gave his life to Christ at the age of seventy. No matter what age, sex, colour, nationality or background, when Jesus is invited into people's lives, miracles happen.

In my walk with Christ, an important milestone was reached when I began to turn my attention away from the problems and looked instead at the circumstances of others. It was a great help in winching me out of a slough of self-pitying sorrows that allowed my fears to run wild.

It was a decision that introduced me to a motley mob in Strangeways Prison, a fifteen-minute walk from the magazine's offices. Following a visit with other Christian men to a church service at the prison (where, not too far in the future, the worst riots in the history of the British penal system would take place, with damage estimated at more than £100m), I became a prison visitor.

With the other Christian men, I sat on a platform with the prison chaplains and discreetly studied the faces of some of the prisoners: the hard-cases, the old lags, the no-hopers. Given the background I came from, I knew that there indeed but for the grace of God. . . .

I've always had a soft spot for life's losers and down-and-outers; those who have been beaten down so many times they can no longer see over the edge of the gutter.

After the service, I spoke to the prison chaplain, Canon Noel Proctor, a small, much-loved Irish man of God, who has seen many a hard villain on his knees in repentance. I asked him how I could become a prison visitor.

A few weeks later, in the company of an experienced prison visitor to show me the ropes, I was placing my signature in a book, against the names of prisoners who had requested a visit. The names ran off the page and onto the next. Due to a lack of prison visitors, many were in for a long wait.

It was the beginning of weekly hour-long visits to five or six prisoners, most of whom lived two to a cell no bigger than about twelve feet by six feet. With some of the prisoners it took at least two or three visits before their caution dropped and I was greeted by a genuinely friendly smile.

An experienced prison visitor told me the prisoners wanted to see if they could depend on my visits before letting down their guard. Many of them had been let down so many times, he added, knowing little else but rejection since childhood that it was hard for them to trust readily. The more I came to know of the prisoners—of their backgrounds, their wives or girl-friends, their childhood, and the crimes they hadn't committed ('honest')—the more I came to look forward to their company.

I avoided any Bible-bashing—that wasn't the point of going, and it can be a tremendous turn-off in their circumstances—but, interestingly, it was they who would raise questions about God. In a way it was inevitable, because once I responded to their questions about me, it would lead to questions about Jesus Christ and the way he had changed my life.

Reflecting on those days, I think our roles became reversed. If my purpose had been to encourage and show kindness to them, it was the likes of Ian, Tony, Terry, Henry, Steve and one or two others, who encouraged and helped me with their good humour, resilience and friendship.

I have to say, and I am not sure what this says about whom, but I felt more at ease with those prisoners than with many a Christian. There was no side, no false image—who could they kid?—and their friendship came from the heart.

It was through Steve, then aged about twenty-four and married with a four-year-old son, that I experienced the incredible joy of seeing a prisoner come to Christ. It happened just minutes before I entered his cell.

Steve's residence in Strangeways came about through the classic route: an unstable, loveless home life; petty crime from early teens; drinking and gambling financed by crime, until, inevitably, he got caught pulling off one burglary too many.

The particular crime that led to Strangeways was planned by Steve's step-father, a hardened criminal, who planned to break into a jewellers. Steve accepted his step-father's invitation to join him. Their haul totalled several thousands of pounds worth of jewellery, but it was a short-lived success.

Police enquiries led them to Steve's step-father, who placed the blame squarely on Steve's shoulders. The whole thing, he said, had been his step-son's idea. Keen to keep her husband out of prison, Steve's mother backed up his story, regardless of the cost to her son.

The judge and the jury believed Steve's mother and step-father. Steve was jailed for seven years, his step-father for two. They were both sent to Strangeways, but to different wings. Soon after I met Steve, he said he had murder in his heart for his mother and step-father.

The sentence had cost him his marriage, and separation from his son, whom he doted upon. He said he wanted revenge, no matter how long it might take. He was driven by hate and bitterness for both his step-father and his mother.

I had first met Steve through visiting his cell-mate. Steve was noticeably indifferent to my visit to the point of rudeness. But during the following weeks he began to respond to a friendly hello, and the week before his cell-mate was due to be transferred to another prison, Steve asked me to visit him.

Some months later, to my surprise, he told me that he had begun attending religious education classes held by Canon Proctor. It gave Steve the biblical guidance and teaching that I was certainly not qualified to give.

Now, that night in his cell, after he told me he had committed his life to Christ, I sat on the edge of a bed opposite as he described how an 'intense heat' had passed through his body, followed by a deep sense of peace. The long-standing anger and bitterness he had felt towards his mother and step-father had gone.

A few weeks later, I received a letter from him in which he described what Christ had achieved in his life. The following is reproduced with his permission:

> Early on in my sentence I couldn't see any future where crime wasn't involved, and now 2 years and 7 months later I've the opportunity to live a good, honest life.
>
> It's amazing the change in my life over the past 12 months. You can probably see that I'm more confident of my abilities and much more relaxed when considering the future.
>
> We both know who to thank for the dramatic change. Two years ago I actually wished my mother to her grave. Today we're both looking forward to Sunday's visit, totally unbelievable two years ago.
>
> I feel much closer to my son these days. But only 12 months ago I was having problems with visits and I only saw him a couple of times over a 12 month period.
>
> I've an awful lot to thank Christ for. Knowing and feeling what I feel now, convinces me that there is a God in this world and he's taken time to repair my life when I thought it was unrepairable.

Steve wrote the letter some months after coming to Christ, from a prison in Full Sutton, near York, where he was transferred to following the outbreak of rioting at Strangeways. The governor, Brendan O'Friel, later described the riots as 'an explosion of evil'. That may well have been true.

A total of twenty-six services and Bible study classes were being held weekly at Strangeways, and the Sunday service was regularly attended by between 600 and 700 prisoners. So many prisoners had come to know Christ in that prison that it was said that 'God moves in Strangeways'. It was in the chapel where, perhaps not surprisingly, the explosion of evil occurred.

Yet despite the brutality and mindless destruction of it all, God was able to use it for his purpose. Some weeks later, I received the prison newsletter, which was devoted to the aftermath of the riot.

On the back page, an article described how the mass transfer of prisoners to other prisons and police station cells throughout the country had led to a wealth of opportunities for the many Christian prisoners to tell others of how God had so dramatically changed their lives.

One notable example involved Martin J., temporarily accommodated in a police station cell which was in such a disgusting state that he asked for—and got—buckets of water and detergent to scrub the graffiti-covered walls.

It led to a friendship between Martin and an astonished police officer who, as a result, began to look to Christ for answers to problems in his own life. The police officer contacted Canon Proctor and they prayed together over the telephone.

Canon Proctor says: 'I had over 600 letters from prayer partners, some of whom said God had scattered the Christian prisoners just as he had scattered the prisoners in Jerusalem.

'Because we so often have our blinkers on, we were not able at the time to see the whole panorama of how perhaps God also used the situation to bring about prison reform. You have to see God in every situation. You have to depend upon the Lord.'

It was through visiting Strangeways that I heard of the way God was reaching men through a remarkable man called Peter. He too was a prison visitor and had been one for many years. He was probably in his mid-sixties, a small, slightly bent, shuffling figure you wouldn't notice standing next to you in a telephone-box.

I didn't get to know him at all. We simply gave each other a nod of recognition as we arrived and left the prison. Another prison visitor, who had taken me on my introductory tour of the cells, knew Peter well, though.

He told me that Peter also made weekly visits to a hostel for down-and-outs, many of them street alcoholics who would end their lives in the gutter. He went there to help the drunks to wash and shave, and simply spend time talking to them.

But he did more than that. He cleaned their shoes, which, by the nature of their owners' existence, would be filthy and dirty, repugnant to the touch.

When the person telling me the story asked Peter why he washed and shaved those men, and even bothered to clean their shoes, he replied: 'To give them dignity.'

It was a story which touched me deeply. I could imagine Jesus Christ in that hostel. In the same way that he washed the feet of the disciples, I think it is precisely what he would do today to identify himself with society's despised and rejected.

It was through the likes of Peter and I first saw for myself the power of Christ at work. Men who not only believe in the word of God, but in using his power.

I saw it also through Bobby, an alcoholic who, close to death, was committed to hospital as his long-suffering wife and children, free of his drunken tyranny after so many years, prepared to leave him.

Doctors told her that if she left him at that point, without her support he was as good as dead. She agreed to stand by him for twelve months and no longer. During that time, Jesus responded when Bobby, in his desperate condition, invited him into his life.

Today he works with his family on one of the roughest council estates in Britain as the pastor of an inner-city mission church. His church, with steel-plated front doors is a constant target of attack. But, despite every possible hurdle, the fellowship is growing, a youth club is flourishing and young kids see the love of Christ in Bobby and his wife and those who work with them, and through that love they are giving their lives to Christ.

I also saw the power of Christ in action through a couple who lost their twelve-year-old son in a road accident. At the hospital, they saw the woman motorist responsible for their son's fatal injuries. She was beside herself with grief. As their son lay dying, they prayed to God that he might comfort her, to ease her deep sorrow.

At their son's funeral, they requested a service of thanksgiving, praising God for the blessings he had given them through their son. This, I felt, is what the power of Christ is all about.

It isn't found in fine words, stirring sermons, cathedral choirs, bishops in splendid robes and mitres, cosy Christian ghettoes and mutual social approval. It is about *doing* things in the power of Christ, expressing love in the power of Christ, to the glory of God.

The people I met through the magazine and personal relationships helped to strengthen me by their example. God used these times to lead me to an awareness of the way he works in people's lives; of what they can achieve, and endure, through his gifts of faith and love.

I was privileged to see the remarkable endurance of Christ-centred love during a trip to Armenia and Georgia some ten months after leaving newspapers and some two years before the break-up of the Soviet Union.

The occasion was a visit to several unregistered Baptist churches in Georgia, which refused to recognise the

State's control of religion, unlike the Russian Orthodox Church, and for their great courage risked the authorities' vicious punishment.

The visit, a clandestine one, had been arranged by the UK office of Friedensstimme, then a West German-based organisation set up to support evangelical churches in the Soviet Union. My role was to write a feature on the visit for the organisation's magazine.

With two UK-based officials, I met unshaven and ill-dressed pastors and leaders of Baptist churches in outlying village areas of Tblisi, the capital. They were burly, granite-hard men who believed in God's word to the letter and even expressed it with a holy kiss on the lips. It is, in accordance with Paul's second letter to the Corinthians, unarguably biblical, but a little unnerving for a Western Christian offering nothing more spiritually passionate than a smile and a hand-shake.

But behind the smiles of sandpaper lips, which would often reveal a glittering display of gold teeth, I experienced in their home fellowships a simplicity of faith and service uncorrupted by the comforts and spiritual liberality of Western society.

Elderly people, with wrinkled leather faces and bodies bent by the rigours of a harsh breadline existence, would walk mountain goat hills to reach a house where, with the host's scant furniture moved to one side, they would sit on hard wooden benches and kneel uncomplainingly on the stone floor for long periods of prayer.

Services would go on all morning and sometimes into the afternoon. Their praise in word and song would continue vigorously to the very last.

These were not two-car family congregations, with 2.3 children, a Sunday roast in the oven, a television in every other room, and little hope in their hearts. These were not the cardboard-cutout Christians who fill the pews of so many Western churches.

They were Christians of the deep spirituality of Ivan Plett who had spent, as I recall, a total of twenty-four years of his thirty-two year marriage in Siberian penal camps for his part in the underground printing and distribution of gospel tracts.

Then there was Anna Chertkova, aged sixty, who was classified by the State as a paranoid schizophrenic, and spent fifteen years in a psychiatric clinic because of her church activities, which included the subversive crime of running a Sunday school. And Viktor Rogalsky, imprisoned for two years in a penal camp in Georgia because he refused to denounce Christ.

We spent many hours in the homes of these people. The offerings of their food, as little as they had, was very touching, and accepting anything less than a full plate risked offending them. They were so humble in their attitude, so gentle in their servant manner and caring in their attention, that I imagine Jesus Christ would have been delighted to have joined their table.

It was an experience that illustrated the stark contrast between the church in the West, which has known too little hardship, and the church in the East, which has known little else.

These suffering Christians knew their suffering Christ, and because of it they knew his strength; through it they endured their times patiently, silently and lovingly.

God blessed me through them. I left Georgia and Armenia with a greater understanding of what Christ's church is really all about. It is the way, I imagine, first-century Christians loved and worshipped God. Holy kiss and all.

Chapter Ten

Be still, and know that I am God (Psalm 46:10).

For the same reason that I put the Jesus Christ sticker on my car rear window and agreed to the interview for the *UK Press Gazette*, I accepted every invitation to talk about Christ. But they were difficult times, and they gave me no sense of joy.

I would stand in front of Christians who wanted to hear powerful words and I didn't have any. The sweat would snake down the sides of my face, seats would shuffle, and, in the stultifying grip of nervousness, I would lose my thoughts, and I would stagger through, with great relief, to the end.

I could only tell them about the kind of person I had been, what I had done in the media circus, and what Christ now meant to me. I couldn't encourage them with what many Christians love to hear—a happy-clappy ending, with bluebirds singing in the spiritual sunset. It wasn't like that.

It wasn't like that because I was still so fearful of what was happening in my life. I still couldn't see beyond my fears and anxieties, because I couldn't see Jesus Christ at my side. Although I prepared and prayed that I would glorify God at these meetings, I would still fall apart inwardly.

And I think that happened because, despite that prayer, I went to those meetings to please the audience and not God. I went for their approval and not his. As ever, I was doing things in my strength and that was the cause of my weakness. It was proving so difficult to give up control of my life.

At these meetings, and many since, I saw Christian men and women in such broken states: spiritually, emotionally and physically. Some would ask me to pray with them at the end of a meeting, and, as we stood there in prayer, I felt very inadequate. I felt I had very little to offer them. But I did know their pain and confusion.

There are many people like us in God's family, who, in their paralysing fears, cling to God's promises as to a liferaft. We pray he will bring about a solution, and, if not, for his strength to continue holding on. We look to the promise of Psalm 91:14–15: '"Because he loves me," says the Lord, "I will rescue him; I will protect him, for he acknowledges my name. He will call upon me, and I will answer him; I will be with him in trouble, I will deliver him and honour him."'

When I think of mankind, I visualise an endless line of wheelchair-bound people. There is little movement, other than strugglings, here and there, of people trying to stand. They are at different stages in their attempts; some are frantic and fearful as they make their first tentative moves; some, gripping the arms of their wheelchairs, are straining with all their might to straighten their bodies; some stumble; some fall in defeat back into their seats to try yet again; while others, at long last, are almost there.

I see these people as men and women committed to

Christ, who, in striving to be more like him, desperately want to overcome their failings and fears. They cry out to him, and yearn from deep within for the day when they will know him in eternity. And through it all, and above all, they continue to try to stand.

The people who remain seated are those who cannot see the deep emptiness and darkness of their lives. They hide their fears in the lies of this world, which causes them to reject and scorn Christ and, inevitably, those who follow him. Through the blindness of their hearts, they are truly crippled.

Through these months I went on accepting invitations to tell of the love of Christ because I too could do nothing but continue to try to stand. But there were times when I seemed far from God indeed. I knew in my head, sure enough, that I had no need to worry, but not in my heart, which is where it matters.

There were also several opportunities to speak to a wider audience through a woman's magazine, Christian newspapers and, for the most part, regional religious radio and television programmes. They went smoothly, but my involvement with two independent TV companies did not, and reminded me of the tabloid tactics I had left behind.

The first was planned as part of a Sunday afternoon series featuring people whose lives had undergone dramatic changes. I agreed to take part, and the interview, which took place in my home, followed a predictable format.

It was decided to wrap up the feature with the TV crew covering an event at a local school the following morning where I was due to help local Gideons hand out copies of the New Testament to schoolchildren.

But the night before the shoot was due to take place, I received a phone call from a reporter, a former colleague on *The People*, who said he wanted to 'mark my card'. He said he had been approached by the programme's researcher and had been offered money to criticise me. Other reporters had been similarly approached. They had already been interviewed in the office of a freelance in Manchester.

As a parting comment, the reporter said: 'There's no fool like a converted fool.' His call caused me to withdraw from the programme, literally minutes before filming was due to take place. I felt sorry for the researcher. I could understand his tactic. At one time I had known his pressures and problems.

The reporter's comment that I was a fool didn't bother me. I knew that the moment I quit newspapers I would be seen as a fool. I didn't feel any anger at being set up either. By then I had stopped looking instinctively for hidden motives in people's words or actions. I felt much happier taking people on the trust of face value.

If I am a 'converted fool', then that suits me. It leaves me open to know and understand others more readily. I would far rather that than shut myself off from those who might need the support and friendship of this fool.

If you are a successful businessman, a penniless student, a concert pianist, a suburban housewife, a brilliant surgeon, a struggling artist, whatever it might be, then be 'a fool for Christ', as the apostle Paul describes himself in 1 Corinthians 4:10. It will strengthen you and help to set you free because you will no longer be imprisoned by the critical comments and opinions of others.

The second brush with a television company came with an invitation to appear on the popular morning chat show, *Kilroy*. The subject under debate was to be the issue of guilt and the way it affects people's lives. I willingly agreed to talk of the guilt I had felt in working, as a Christian, for a newspaper such as *The People*.

On the day, the studio audience consisted of carefully selected individuals whose lives had been affected by guilt resulting from tragic circumstances. Some of the accounts were sad in the extreme and the host, Robert Kilroy, skilfully and sympathetically manipulated them to talk in detail of their experiences. One woman, in responding to questions about the cause of her guilt, was upset to the point of tears.

Kilroy moved from one person to another, and finally came to a halt by a man sitting in front of me. It was a reporter from the *News of the World*. I knew his byline well, and although we had met briefly during my newspaper days in *The People*'s London office, I hadn't recognised him.

Kilroy quizzed him on the sensational stories he had written and of their effect on people's lives. Didn't he feel really terrible about what he had done? Surely he felt guilty? The reporter felt otherwise and attempted to justify his stories.

Turning quickly to me, Kilroy suddenly placed the microphone under my nose to ask: 'What do you think of what he's done?' I replied that I wasn't there to criticise the reporter. It clearly wasn't what Kilroy wanted to hear.

Given my views about the gutter press, which I had expressed to one of his researchers, he was clearly expecting me to round on the reporter.

Without another word, he turned on his heel and crossed the studio floor to a more obliging guest. It was obvious that both the reporter and I had been set up, with even our seating conveniently arranged to facilitate some face-to-face confrontational television.

It was tacky tabloid television. One or two people had clearly been distressed as their psychological wounds and scars were revealed and prodded for the public's entertainment. As with tabloid newspapers, controversy is the lifeblood of such television programmes, with opposing factions brought together and wound up to unleash on each other as much aggression and hostility as possible.

The importance of the subject and the views of the guests are of no importance, other than for their controversy rating. As in so much of the media, the plan is to set controversy against controversy to attract readers/viewers, to attract advertisers, to attract profits.

The currently popular alibi used by tabloid press editors in particular in defence of their actions is that readers have 'a right to know'. It implies that if readers are not informed of some sensational revelation they are somehow being denied their 'rights', as if it were enshrined in democratic freedom.

For a tabloid editor to make such a claim is a deliberate distortion of the meaning of the word to disguise his real interest: circulation. When gutter press editors turn on their critics with this so-noble argument, they are not concerned with anything else, least of all the 'rights' of readers.

It is unlikely that even gutter press readers themselves would put claim to such a 'right', any more than a buyer of a pornographic magazine could rationally claim that he has a 'right' to such material.

The excesses of the gutter press in playing on the basest of human traits are indeed as damaging as pornography in undermining society, although their consequences are far more subtle, almost subliminal, in their long-term consequences.

They encourage cynicism, mistrust and suspicion; they exploit the weak and vulnerable; they delight in the misfortunes and disgrace of others; they mock those who are unable to hit back; they not only damage the people they attack but, ironically, their readers also. They too become victims.

Some editors have publicly claimed to consider the consequences to innocent family and relatives of publishing sensational material. That is not unlike a bank robber claiming he considers the cost to the bank before holding it up. To operate successfully, gutter press editors cannot allow themselves to be restrained by such thoughts.

Their considerations do not extend beyond a story's possible legal repercussions to the paper; all other matters are of little importance. For this reason, a self-monitoring media cannot work, any more than a pit bull terrier can suppress its fighting instincts.

Nothing less totalitarian than the closure of a newspaper for a fixed period would succeed in reforming editorial policies. When publishers and shareholders are threatened with a loss of profits they will then begin seriously to review their news coverage and newsgathering tactics.

But its implementation would depend on the most determined political will of a united parliament—a likelihood made extremely unlikely due to the enormous corporate and political interests in the existence of a 'free' media. Moreover, it would be at complete odds with the democratic principles of a free society.

Legislative suppression of the gutter press is not the answer. The answer lies within a spiritual trans-formation of society, not in the Houses of Parliament.

And a true, lasting transformation can only come through Jesus Christ.

Until that takes place, the media's critics, and indeed those concerned by the state of mankind at large—from politicians, social and welfare organisations, and police authorities to educationalists, magistrates and the man in the street—are whistling vainly in the wind.

I am not at all sure it is now possible, in fact, for controls to be imposed upon the tabloid media, even if desired. Their power has become too great, the political commitment too weak and public opinion too indifferent.

The ideal solution is for people simply to stop supporting the gutter press, but then this is a naïve hope in a Western culture so deeply hooked on a news agenda of sex and scandal.

The gutter press format eases the dullness and emptiness of existence for so many people who are unaware that their ghoulish and voyeuristic interests in the tragedies of other people's lives mirror the meaninglessness of their own.

The downward spiral of the tabloid media has become ever more marked in recent years and its knock-on effect has been to cause a deterioration in the standards of the media at large, which has been unable to ignore the market influence of the tabloids.

Evidence of its consequences is seen in the incident involving the American television network, NBC, which confessed to faking a petrol tank explosion in an attempt to prove that a motor company's pick-up truck was dangerous. Media analysts claimed that prestigious networks such as NBC were being 'forced' to 'cut corners and go down-market' to compete with the increasingly popular tabloid scandal journalism on cable television.

There have been two similar examples of 'down-marketing' in the UK recently. In a front-page story, a newspaper gave a detailed account of the way in which Tory MP Stephen Milligan died in a bizarre sexual experiment. The paper described precisely how it was done, including naming the sexual stimulant and manner in which it was taken. It would have given every encouragement to other sexual misfits to carry out similar perversions.

The same newspaper, in the same week, published on its front page a photograph of a radio/television producer, who had been cut out of the wreckage of her car, being carried into an ambulance. She appeared unconscious and her bandaged head was heavily stained with blood. Her condition in the story was described as 'very serious'. How distressing that photograph would have been to her family and friends.

The newspaper concerned wasn't *The Sun* or the *Daily Mirror*, or the *News of the World* or *The People*, but *The Daily Telegraph*. *The Times*, too, has in recent years markedly lowered its reporting standards in order to court the popular market. The so-called quality press plays the same game as the gutter press in exposing the sexual infidelities and perversions of others, but they do it through the columns of their literary supplements by serialising the biographies of some politician, artist or Royal.

Because such articles are pretensiously dressed in a dinner jacket and bow-tie, they are read eagerly by people who would claim to be shocked by the gutter press. But they all work to the same end: the corruption and debasement of humanity. And such is the influence of the tabloids that quality newspapers now publish glossy horoscope supplements to boost circulation. They may look sniffily down their noses at the gutter press, but in reality they sup from the same spoon.

The evidence of the spread of the tabloids' influence can also be seen in certain women's magazines which condone sexual promiscuity and adultery, and scornfully deride traditional male-female relationships; and in teenage magazines which give graphic details of sexual techniques and see no harm in homosexual and lesbian experimentation. As with the tabloids' agony aunts, they give unqualified advice to the emotionally frail and immature, who, tragically, are only too willing to believe what they read.

All contribute in their own dangerous ways and at different levels to the destruction of relationships and, inevitably, the undermining of family values, which are crucial to a stable society.

I was asked recently whether I believe the media to be the Antichrist. No, I don't, but I do believe that the media is central to Satan in his constant strategy of separating mankind from God. He knows the weaknesses of editors and publishers and how to manipulate their fears, and does so with every edition.

If it is true that people get the government they deserve, they also get the media they deserve. The tragedy is that Christians are so unwilling to stand in opposition to what is wrong and destructive in the media. It is easy to understand how overwhelmed one can feel by the negative and harmful nonsense spewed out daily through newspapers, magazines, television, films and videos, but that can never be an excuse if we stand for Christ.

Many, I think, might be surprised to learn how effective a letter of complaint can be. Although the response, if one is received at all, suggests such a letter has made not the slightest scrap of difference, it can in fact have a surprisingly positive effect.

At a recent Christian men's breakfast, the speaker, an executive of a regional television company, said that when an actor in a top-rating soap used a blasphemous word four Christians wrote in to complain. No more than that, but it was enough for a memo to be issued to the scriptwriters making it clear that the word was not to be used again.

When Christians pray and act, things happen. When they don't the enemy gains ground. Even if you feel that you are the only Christian in the world who cares enough to voice a complaint, then carry on. As Christians we stand to glorify God, whether we stand above or not.

It is also important to praise a newspaper or television station when they get it right. Even editors need to be loved, and a letter congratulating a newspaper, whether national, regional or weekly, is likely to encourage a similar story another time. A positive and supportive response to a story or television programme is just as important as one that justly criticises.

About twelve months after leaving newspapers, I received an imperial summons from my bank. I attended a solemn meeting with a brusque young executive in a floral tie who was clearly intent on high office. Sadistically, he informed me of the cashflow figure that had zipped its way through my account during my last year with *The People*. I was impressed. He then compared it with the size of my overdraft. He was not impressed.

He said that since leaving newspapers, I hadn't exactly covered myself in glory. They were his precise words, but it left me wondering how he knew my spiritual condition. In return for his time, I spent the best part of ten seconds giving a summary of my business prospects and anticipated income. To my surprise, the bank agreed to extend my overdraft.

Three months later, though, with the interest on my credit cards in free-fall and my bank manager requesting my passport, it was necessary to obtain a hefty bank loan to reschedule a five-figure debt load. I thought things couldn't get much worse. But they did.

I had to part company with the Christian trade magazine, which took my income down to zero. Sue, still child-minding the Wild Bunch, was now holding the financial fort single-handed and was no doubt extremely worried by my resignation from a Christian publication, although she quietly battled on.

I rented an office about the size of a broom cupboard, part of which actually included a very cold disused lift shaft. I produced a promotional brochure I couldn't afford and sent it out to local companies who might conceivably be in need of a media and public relations consultant. I then sat in the office, staring at the telephone.

In the meantime, I followed up a chance meeting I had had some weeks earlier with the managing director of a small book production company well known in the Christian book trade. It led to discussions for the launch of another Christian book trade magazine, this time covering the European religious book market.

His enthusiasm for the project was tremendous news. From the date of the first issue I would be employed by his company. The bad news was that the launch date of *The European Christian Bookseller* would be the Christian book trade's prestigious annual convention, and this—along with the start of my salary—was some six months away.

With the phone so silent that I thought it had been cut off, there was not the slightest prospect of any kind of immediate media work to pay bills which were six feet high and rising. I sat in my miserable broom cupboard office staring miserably through a miserable grimy window on a miserable early winter's afternoon and yearned for the bliss of a holiday in the sun.

A day or two later, the office resounded to the sound of the phone ringing. It was from the offices of an English-speaking magazine in the Algarve, Portugal. A female voice said the publisher's wife had read an article about—yes, the gutter press hack who had found God—in a women's magazine, through whose office my phone number had been traced.

She wanted to know if I knew of a British journalist who might be interested in editing the magazine. I most certainly did. Five minutes later, it had been agreed that I would meet the publisher during an imminent business trip to London.

I was astonished by God's remarkable intervention. In one move, he had thrown me a much-needed financial lifeline and booked me a spell in the heat of southern Portugal. Coincidence? Not a chance. Since coming to Christ I had experienced too many of these 'coincidences' to believe in them. As someone once said: 'When I pray "coincidences" occur, when I don't, they don't.'

My appointment as editor of the magazine, which also offered a permanent move for my family to the Algarve, was an eleventh-hour rescue typical of God's caring intervention. Immense financial pressures were eased considerably overnight and I flew out to the Algarve, to an apartment in Portamao, a company car and a deal which allowed me to fly home for one week in every four.

The invitation to move on a permanent basis to the Algarve was declined primarily for family reasons, but also because I believed the editorship of a Christian book trade magazine was more meaningful than a lotus-eating life with totally insane Portuguese motorists who had me at the top of their hit list.

I returned permanently to the UK the following March for the magazine's successful launch at the Christian Booksellers' Convention. The popularity of the magazine was instant. Within two or three issues, the advertising base was becoming firmly established. The subscription take-up rate, in the UK and overseas, continued to confirm its popularity throughout the industry.

I came to understand a good deal more of the Christian book trade industry—particularly of booksellers who, in many cases, were barely earning a salary in their enthusiasm to get Christian books into the high street. Many, in middle-age or having taken early retirement, had stepped out in faith and little else to follow God's leading.

As someone who has been encouraged and comforted countless times, and very much continues to be so, by the spiritual wisdom and understanding of the likes of Charles Spurgeon and Martyn Lloyd-Jones, C.S.Lewis, Charles Swindoll and Selwyn Hughes, I believe that Christian booksellers need to be reassured of the importance of their work.

They are very much in a mission field, and a frontline one at that. I have known a number of men, particularly prisoners, who, in the quiet of their cells, have come to Christ through the published testimony of a broken-nosed villain who committed his life to Christ.

Churches too have a crucial role to play in promoting sound Christian books, but so many fall down sadly. A dust-covered bookstall at the back of the church isn't good enough. Most Christian books help to strengthen and sustain the Christian and the Christian family. They should be used by church leaders as a significant factor in any evangelistic strategy.

I heard it said recently that Christians who rarely read Christian books are unlikely to spend much time reading their Bible. At first it seemed a strange thing to say, but as I reflected upon it, perhaps not. How sad then that only 10% of this country's 10 million churchgoers visit Christian bookshops.

Chapter Eleven

Stop trusting in man,
who has but a breath in his nostrils.
Of what account is he? (Isaiah 2:22).

Every now and then a relatively stable time of work
and income was provided by God as a plateau of rest
and recovery. The launch of *The European Christian
Bookseller* and the months ahead was such a time,
when the degree of financial security was at least sufficient for my bank manager to return my passport.

The magazine was successful, with Christian publishers giving it their unanimous support. Its subscription rate also proved its popularity in what is a low-
budget niche market within a niche market.

However, as production was not geared to more
economical computerised technology, the costs/profits
ratio caused the publishing company continuing concern until there was no alternative but to close the
magazine down just one issue short of its second birthday.

The news of its closure came about a month before
Christmas, I carried on smiling and joking and agree-

ing when Christian brothers told me not to worry because God was in control. I prayed that he really was, as inside the well-remembered fears ripped into me again.

At these times, I would agonise over what I could do to stand stronger. I felt ashamed of my lack of faith, and yet I seemed unable to do anything to help myself. In my darkness, I saw no hope, no purpose, and it was during these many times that I felt so grateful for God's patience with me. I could only seek his forgiveness and keep praying every morning for his strength.

I felt this way even though I had long understood that what was happening in my life was essential to God's plans for me. I knew the person I had been. I knew that only God could bring about the changes necessary if, as I said, I desired to be more like Christ. I understood and accepted the wisdom of Job 5:17—'Blessed is the man whom God corrects; so do not despise the discipline of the Almighty.'

I knew he would not load me down with more than I coud bear (1 Corinthians 10:13), and that encouraged me. Perversely, I gained confidence from the circumstances I was in because I knew God would not put me into any situation I could not endure, and for this promise I thanked him.

I went back time and again to the many wonderful promises of Psalms, Isaiah and Jesus himself (Matthew 6:25–34), and I knew of God's might and power and compassion through Moses, Abraham, Joseph, Joshua, David, Isaiah, Daniel and so many other great men of God. I knew of their weaknesses, and how they had let God down, and that encouraged me too.

At these times, I tried to burn the truths of his word into my head and heart, and this kept me moving. I knew I believed God's promises. I just had to keep hanging on. I would put my Bible to one side and take on the day.

But then another pressure would occur. Perhaps it would be something quite incidental, but it would be enough to bring me down to a point where, fatally, I would allow all the circumstances around me to pull me apart. These pressures invariably came through somebody close to me. Satan really knows how to put the boot in.

I was rather like headstrong, over-the-top Peter—my favourite disciple, I think—when he stepped out of the boat at Jesus's command and walked on the water, until he allowed himself to feel the force of the wind and the waves and began to sink. That was me.

I couldn't keep my focus on Christ. I allowed the power of his words as I read my Bible to desert me. Then—and this is where Satan is brilliantly devious—I would feel a deep guilt for allowing myself to be so weak, which would add to the torment. Not only was I failing in business as a providing husband and father, but as a Christian who couldn't put into practice the teachings of the Christ he followed.

This all-round failure would hit my sense of self-worth badly and I would be thrown back into the darkness of those sleepless nights and early mornings with my Bible in the kitchen. It was these times with God that brought me through each day. There was no one else I could turn to. I cannot describe the sense of despair and loneliness and isolation of those days, of which there were many.

An executive of a leading Christian business suggested that I should somehow find a way to continue with the publication of *The European Christian Bookseller*. It was something the trade needed, he said.

In principle, it was a good idea, but the question was: who would source the capital? I knew most of the decision-makers in Christian publishing and there was no one with the interest, the vision or the available money to make it work.

Yet I had to do something. The only option was to publish it myself. By using desktop publishing technology, changing the format from A4 to tabloid and selling the advertising myself, the production costs of what was to arise out of the ashes of a trade publication now known as *The Christian Bookseller* were reduced by more than 50%.

A front-page dummy faxed to major publishers was well received. Their support, which was crucial, was promised. Suddenly, overnight, I was in business, producing the first issue of the relaunch from the dining room of my house where the Wild Bunch were still shooting up the town.

By the end of the fourth week, the advertising revenue target had been reached, and the editorial pages were on schedule for its arrival at the Christian Booksellers' Convention just a few weeks away.

On the day before the convention opened, I loaded bundles of the first issue into the back of my car and drove from the printers in Liverpool to the convention in Bournemouth. Two hundred and fifty miles or so down the motorway, they were unloaded into the convention centre with the help of a young Christian who, with a camera swinging around his neck, was there to take some snaps for the next issue, sell subscriptions and generally give me support. It had been an extremely tight schedule, but it had been met.

The overall comment on the new-look trade newspaper was encouragingly positive. I spent my time at the convention rounding up news and features for the next issue, happily unaware that my joy was going to be short-lived indeed.

Even at the convention, gentle hints were dropped by some of the smaller publishers, whose advertising support was the difference between a working profit and disaster, that, with convention promotion money now spent up, their budgets couldn't promise regular support.

I drove away from Bournemouth in a dark mood which matched the office I'd moved into on the basement floor of a massive, red-brick building, a former Co-op head office, in a slum property area of Manchester, which had been converted into office units.

My office, twelve foot by twelve foot breezeblock-walled area without windows, had some colourful neighbours, which included the Animal Liberation Front, a Vietnamese Boat People support association, a lesbian magazine editorial office, a black agit-prop group and a man who made cuckoo clocks in the 'office' opposite.

To the background noise of his electric saws and drills, the news that I feared was confirmed with every phone call to the smaller Christian publishers. The support of the major companies, which in Christian publishing totals just three, plus a wholesale distributor/bookstore chain, wasn't enough.

The chances of *The Christian Bookseller* reaching a second issue were fading hourly. I certainly didn't have the cashflow necessary to float the newspaper until publishers' fortunes—and marketing budgets—improved. The success of the first issue had raised hopes of a more secure financial future, to the joy of a family long used to a belt running out of notches to tighten.

It had been about three years and seven months

since my departure from newspapers, and I was still reassuring Sue that everything would work out. It clearly hadn't proved to be the case, and my claims that God would provide for us gave harsh comfort.

In addition to believing that I was failing my family, I now also felt a deep sense of guilt for letting down publisher friends who had given every financial and moral support, and were really keen for the newspaper to do well. The sense of guilt and failure I felt in letting people down seemed overwhelming.

With all the difficulties that had been met and endured through God's grace and strength, I had on more than one occasion believed that I had come to a point where I had the faith to overcome all obstacles. How wrong I was.

The familiar crisis was this time more than financial. There was also some considerable concern over our eldest son, Sam. Diagnosed a diabetic shortly before I quit newspapers, he seemed to be having trouble in maintaining his blood sugar level, which led to a couple of hospital emergencies.

Toby, my son by my first marriage, had developed a serious thyroid gland dysfunction which made it impossible for him to continue working. His condition was made worse by an allergy to the standard medication.

Alexandra, my eldest daughter by my first marriage and a single parent of two, developed epilepsy. Living alone, she had had two serious accidents following fits, which had been brought on, in part, by various domestic pressures.

Since I had handed in my resignation there hadn't appeared to be any respite from financial, professional, domestic or spiritual difficulties, and sometimes all simultaneously. But this time was to prove the most devastating.

And yet, although my lack of faith seemed to keep God far from me, he was, as ever, there at my side, shoring me up and giving me encouragement in a very practical and most unlikely way.

His presence came to me through a former drug addict—a young man who had committed his life to Christ and who was then trying to establish himself as a photographer. He was the one who came with me to the Bournemouth convention, and although he was going through a very tough time himself, he would come into the office to offer what help he could.

He would arrive, swathed in smiles and his motor-bike gear. There wasn't much he could do to help, really—he was no writer, as he knew, and cold-calling for advertising he abhorred—but we spent a lot of time praying. When I look back I think God must have been delighted at what he saw: the former gutter press hack and the former drug addict in worship of the Lord Jesus Christ, desperately praying for his help in the battle of their different circumstances.

How melodramatic it all sounds, but it was in those moments that for an instant, as we had our arms around each other in our tears, I sensed the very real presence of Jesus Christ—with his arms around both of us.

We have a most remarkable Father. Who, as Job asked, 'can understand the thunder of his power'? And who can understand the power of his love?

I have experienced the presence of his loving power in many ways: the right word of encouragement and hope at the right time from another Christian; a message during a church service which the Holy Spirit reinforces; a sense of calm that can follow a time of prayer with him, or through his word; or the unmistakeable force of his presence and guidance when a particular line or verse is clearly understood.

It has been my experience that the degree of God's intervention depends on the precise degree of help necessary—no more or no less. He wastes no effort. Sometimes, as in those times of prayer with the former drug addict, when he hears the cries of our heart, he will embrace us through the presence of another. I have known this kind of intervention a few times, but only on one other occasion so dramatically.

It took place during a meeting with a man whose conversion to Christ was so extraordinary that it had been suggested I should ghost his biography. As we sat in my house and I asked him many questions about his background, I suddenly found it very difficult to continue.

I couldn't shift the heavy sense of despair over all that seemed to be going wrong. My mind went blank and I couldn't go on. Suddenly I found myself telling him something of my past and what was happening in the present.

We prayed together for some time, and soon the dark mood of despair was gone. It turned out to be a day of tremendous fellowship with a Christian brother, who after committing his life to Christ, had known much fear, anxiety and rejection.

Much later that day, at the end of our meeting, I realised how it had reinforced the truth that God is aware of our needs before we ourselves know them, for our meeting had been arranged some ten days earlier. But God knew what lay ahead; he knew my needs well in advance, and he was there, through that brother, to give me the hope and encouragement I so badly needed.

It was also a meeting that taught me more of the endless mystery of his ways. For that man, until Christ came into his life, had sexually abused a number of children—offences for which he had been imprisoned.

Once I would have taken delight in working for his public disgrace through the columns of *The People*, but now, like me, he was in Christ, 'a new creation' (2 Corinthians 5:17), and we were able to come together in Christ and console each other. How wonderful indeed that our thoughts are not God's thoughts, and that our ways are not his ways (Isaiah 55:8).

That *I* was able to be a source of encouragement is the third point in this experience of a God who is always so economical and purposeful in his moves. This man, who had found difficulty in knowing the full love of some Christians, said he felt so grateful to God that I had welcomed him as a Christian brother. He knew the shame of what he had done, and he knew that God had forgiven him, but some Christians, even within his own church, couldn't find it in their hearts to express what God had given freely.

Looking back on that time, I praise God again for the hope and strength he gave me through that man, through whom, in his willingness to accept the rejection of other Christians, I also came to understand more of the meaning of God's grace. We do indeed have an amazing God.

As I continued in vain my attempts to rescue *The Christian Bookseller*, with each day adding to the hopelessness of my efforts, I continued to allow the pressures to get to me, until I reached a point of paralysing indecision. My mental state was such that I was unable to decide what was important and what wasn't; whom I should speak to and whom I shouldn't. My fears were in complete control.

Where now was the reporter and news editor whose confidence and arrogance could take on the world single-handed? Where was the man ready to make too many decisions, irrespective of their consequences to others? He was certainly not in that place that day. Instead, there was a man disabled by circumstances which he allowed to overwhelm him, and, because of it, believed he was cracking up.

I recall that I actually wanted to break down so that I could have an alibi for all that was going wrong. It would have been a cowardly exit, but I had had enough of all the pressures and problems that seemed interminable. Although I felt I couldn't hold myself together any longer, the thread simply wouldn't snap.

I phoned my neighbour David S., who worked on the other side of Manchester, asking him to help me. He responded immediately and soon he was by my side trying to guide my thoughts, to clear my head, but I could do nothing but walk round the office, permitting my fears to keep me in a blinding panic.

We drove home, and I went to bed for another bad night full of fears which drove me yet again to Psalms and Isaiah and other random passages annotated on the fly leaf of my Bible which, at so many different times, had strengthened me.

The despair of those nights took on an appalling intensity when I began to think that God couldn't possibly be with me, because there had been so *many* nights like this. I had prayed so *much*, I had tried to follow his teachings, yet they were still happening. Where was God? What was he doing?

I felt so alone one night that I went into the bedroom of my daughter, Elizabeth, then aged three, and held her body close to mine, hoping that I would somehow receive from her the strength I needed from a God who seemed unwilling to help. Then I would return to bed and simply lie, in great fear, clutching my Bible to my chest, as if I could somehow press its truth into my heart.

By now my eldest daughters, Sophie and Jessica, were aware that our difficulties had been caused by my resignation, but they accepted our changed circumstances without question—I think they knew I didn't have the answers.

We live in the kind of suburb where the local brass band has a string section—turbo BMWs, ponies in the stable and villas in Spain, that kind of suburb—and they were now growing up to realise that a dad who quits his jobs because of someone they sometimes hear about in religious education classes must be round the bend.

Sometimes, when they brought new friends around, I sensed that I was being given a very uncertain once-over. Was I going to produce a banner declaring that the end of the world is nigh and march around the kitchen?

It was one of the toughest things, not being able, as a matter of normal household expense, to buy my family the clothes they wanted. But they've always been clothed and well fed. We've also tried to give them all the loving support possible, which is better for them than stuffing a £20 note in their purses—even though they might sometimes claim otherwise.

I hope they have come to understand that the woman neighbour who told them I had resigned from newspapers, not because I had become a Christian, but because I'd had a nervous breakdown, had got it wrong. With the patient, sympathetic tone one usually adopts when trying to explain the quantum theory to a half-wit, the neighbour told me herself what she had done, believing she had rendered us a tremendous kindness.

It illustrates the immense chasm between Christians and non-believers. As Paul writes in 1 Corinthians 1:18: 'For the message of the cross is foolishness to those who are perishing, but to us who are being saved it is the power of God.'

At the breakfast table one morning, Sophie, concerned at the condition I was in, suggested I started taking sleeping pills. Sue, equally concerned, had made the same suggestion some days earlier. I longed to have the oblivion of a deep night's sleep, but I couldn't agree to that solution.

If at that time I had taken sleeping pills, it would have been like conceding defeat. I would have been admitting, in effect, that I didn't trust God to protect me and bring me through my circumstances. In taking the situation out of his control, I believed would have left myself even more vulnerable to the attacks of Satan. I would have been weakened, and I was weak enough, so I had to hold on to God and the proof of what I knew of him through my experiences and his word and the times of prayer.

Early morning times with him became more and more crucial. They were the key to surviving the days. On some days, exhausted, drained and depressed, when I had pleaded in the early morning for God's strength to carry on, I would sense a warm, acknowledging stirring of the Holy Spirit at their end, as if to say, 'Well done.' God, I believe, was letting me know that he was with me, as close as ever. I just had to keep hanging on.

Those early morning conversations with God have become essential to the day. Without them, the day is out of balance and I feel incomplete.

If you are new to Christ, start the habit of beginning your day with God. I have found the earlier the better.

There is a stillness in the early hours, before anything stirs, that helps to create a sense of quiet and closeness. You will find it becomes a special time to you; a time of renewing and strengthening, and on which your day will depend.

It is all the more so if you have come from a background of particular darkness. Satan does not give up on the holiest of Christians. While God rejoices in re-establishing a relationship with you, Satan seethes with fury at losing you. He will not give up his attempts to bring you down in the most devious and ruthless ways imaginable.

I think we need to remember that Satan's interest in us is incidental. His one aim is to hurt God. That is where his true interests lie. And he knows that the only way he can do that is by destroying the people God loves so much, and for whom, because he loves us so much, he willingly put Jesus Christ on the cross. We are, if you like, God's Achilles' heel.

It is precisely for this reason that we need, as Paul urges in Ephesians 6:11, to 'put on the full armour of God so that you can take your stand against the devil's schemes. For our struggle is not against flesh and blood, but against the rulers, against the authorities, against the powers of this dark world and against the spiritual forces of evil in the heavenly realms.'

Knowing the protection of God's armour comes through spending time every day with God and immersing ourselves in the Bible which, Paul goes on, is 'the sword of the Spirit, which is the word of God', and adds that we should 'pray in the Spirit on all occasions with all kinds of prayers and requests. With this in mind, be alert and always keep on praying for all the saints.'

If you are suffering great difficulties at the moment

and need to know God's strength, go to him and spend time in prayer. It isn't time wasted. Whatever you do, don't try to stand in your own strength. You will put yourself outside God's protection, and that is fatal.

Without any hope of bringing out the next issue of *The Christian Bookseller*, I began, as a last-ditch hope, looking for a 'white knight': a businessman who would have the capital and interest to make it work.

At the suggestion of a friend, I phoned someone I had met at a Christian businessmen's weekend. No, was the reply, he couldn't help, but he did mention the name of a businessman whose acquaintance, 'coincidentally', I had renewed at the booktrade convention launch of *The Christian Bookseller* some weeks earlier. In fact, I recalled, he expressed admiration of its design and content.

I phoned him and we spent some time talking. He had once held a senior position in the Reed group, one-time owners of Mirror Group Newspapers, my former employers, so we had a mutual area of interest.

As I answered his questions about the production costs of *The Christian Bookseller*, his attitude slowly changed during our lengthy conversation from one of courteous disinterest to positive enthusiasm. My attitude slowly changed from one of total despair to sheer joy.

The businessman's main activity was staging a major Christian trade exhibition, which had been successfully established for some while, and the idea of returning to publishing increasingly attracted his interest.

By the end of our phone conversation, he had invited me for a meeting the following afternoon at his office in Buckinghamshire. During that meeting, he made an offer, a nominal sum, to buy *The Christian Bookseller*. I happily accepted, and agreed to continue as editor at a salary which, for a long time, represented a working salary.

In the space of twenty-four hours, God had over-turned what had seemed a most impossible situation. Once more, at the eleventh hour, if not the fifty-ninth minute of the eleventh hour, he had brought about a complete reversal of circumstances. As always, I felt ashamed that my faith in him had been so lacking; that, as I believed, I had let him down, and, as always, I took my shame to him for his forgiveness.

The Christian Bookseller, in the hands of a com-pany with the necessary financial resources, manage-ment expertise and commitment, quickly established its role in the Christian booktrade. From my basement bunker, I originated and wrote the news and features to fill a minimum sixteen-page publication.

It was a hectic, enjoyable time. However, nine months after its launch, my involvement with *The Christian Bookseller* came to an end.

But this time there was to be no concern or anxiety. Instinctively, I went to God's word and began leafing through its pages. They stopped at Isaiah 46. My eyes fell on the fourth verse: 'Even to your old age and grey hairs I am he, I am he who will sustain you. I have made you and I will carry you; I will sustain you and I will rescue you.'

The words filled me with cheer and calm. I con-tinued leafing through the pages of the Old Testament. This time the page came to rest at Habakkuk, the book of a minor prophet which I think I have read no more than once. Here, my eyes chanced on the last part of chapter 3, verses 17–19, which tell us to praise God in all circumstances; that although the crops fail and there are no sheep in the pen or cattle in the stalls, 'yet I will rejoice in the Lord, I will be joyful in God my Saviour. The Sovereign Lord is my strength; he makes my feet like the feet of a deer, he enables me to go on the heights.'

This I did—I praised him with all my heart—and with the same certainty that I knew God had spoken to me through the verse in Isaiah, I knew that he was now speaking to me through Habakkuk. Regardless of my circumstances and the pressures, I was to rejoice in him and continue to praise his name. Then, through his grace, I would be enabled to 'go on the heights'—overcome any obstacle—with the sure-footed confidence of a deer.

Over the next few days, I experienced the supernatural peace that Paul describes in his letter to the Philippians—chapter 4, verses 6–7—in which he urges them not to be anxious about anything 'but in everything, by prayer and petition, with thanksgiving, present your requests to God. And the peace of God, which transcends all understanding, will guard your hearts and your minds in Christ Jesus.'

I came to understand for the first time the crucial importance of praising God in all things, irrespective of all considerations and circumstances. Through God's peace and joy, I began to experience a release from the intense pressures of the circumstances around. I felt no concern or anxiety for the future.

What I was experiencing, through God's blessing, was the power of a trust that came from the heart and not from the head. It was an inexplicable calm I knew could have no other source.

Chapter Twelve

The fears that drove me for so many years had their origins in a working-class childhood and adolescence that caused me to believe I lacked the ability to succeed in journalism. From a local newspaper career that began on lies and bluff, I stumbled on as best I could in those early years, learning how to smother and disguise a deep sense of inadequacy, and yearning for the approval of others.

It was that need for approval that motivated me as a reporter. I wanted the biggest stories, the best bylines, because they earned the admiration and approval of people I admired. Approval made me feel good because it made me feel secure. It gave me reassurance and comfort that kept my awareness of my inadequacies in check.

I was ready to work all hours on any story and do anything that was necessary for the pat on the back that success would bring. Failure, on the other hand, unleashed all the insecurities that caused me to feel threatened and afraid. I would believe I had disappointed people and they might cease to approve of me.

The same insecurities manipulated me as northern news editor. But ironically the success of my efforts to please executive colleagues came to be seen as a threat, and led to the very thing I drove myself to avoid: their disapproval and rejection.

Like a confused and hurt child who couldn't understand why he'd been punished, I responded by making every effort to get bigger and better stories still. I did so with an arrogance and supreme self-confidence which succeeded only cutting me further adrift. My fears of isolation and rejection deepened, and hardened into anger and bitterness. I believed I had nowhere to turn, no one I could trust, nothing I could do other than battle on single-handed, full of self-sustaining pride and contempt for my executive colleagues.

I was in this state of mind when, after a runaway diversion to Los Angeles, I stepped down as northern news editor and returned to the road as a reporter, looking for the honesty and simplicity that for me could no longer exist. Instead, I found myself in a professional vacuum, uncertain of what I was doing with my life or what lay ahead.

It was at this point that Christ Jesus came out of the shadows of my life. In his divine plan for me since the beginning of time—Ephesians 1:4, 'For he chose us in him before the creation of the world to be holy and blameless in his sight'—God had been moving the scenery into place for this moment in my life. All that had happened up to that point had been engineered by God to bring me to an acknowledgement of him and the establishing of my relationship with him.

The joy I then experienced was the joy of understanding that Christ Jesus loves me, irrespective of my shortcomings and inadequacies. It is a love with no strings attached. It doesn't depend on what I can give or achieve, my professional status or intellect. The loving, caring and compassionate Jesus who gave his life for me became everything. My job, the salary, the expenses, became as nothing.

It is a love that placed itself upon a cross and endured the most agonising death in full payment for my sins. Through Christ's crucifixion I was redeemed. Through his death, I was born again, and, in that re-birth, I became a child of God who will one day be with him in his perfect kingdom, in the paradise of his light and glory, praising him for ever.

It was this agape love—this self-sacrificing love—for someone like me that caused uncontrollable tears to flow as I committed my life to Christ Jesus. It was this divine, amazing love that made sense of my life, that filled me with an overwhelming awareness that every-thing was all right. It made me feel clean and filled me with a sense of wholeness and purpose.

In receiving his forgiveness for my sins, I also received his unqualified approval for ever. And, as Christ *is* perfect love, there can be no fear of rejection. To reject those he loves would be to reject himself. Incredibly, we can do nothing in return for this love other than to seek his forgiveness for our sins and invite him into our hearts.

The fears that dominated me are common to men and women who, in the absence of God, are created by their fears and destroyed by them. It is why, in the words of Henry Thoreau, the nineteenth-century poet and essayist, 'The mass of men live lives of quiet des-peration.' In that desperation, people attempt to quell their fears in the the pursuit of ambition and material acquisitions to reinforce an image of status, strength and power. The more we acquire, the still more we must acquire to appease the fears that drive us. We are not freed by wealth and status, but enshackled and dragged down by them.

And as our worth is, by this world's standards, measured by the degree of our power and possessions, it must follow that, stripped of title and trappings, we are worthless. But let us thank God that indeed his ways are not the ways of this world. He does not measure our worth by the size of our bank account or corporate seniority.

God loves us because we are his creation, his children, and he wants nothing more than that we seek to establish a right and loving relationship with him through our Saviour, the Lord Jesus Christ. Compared to this world's standards, his love is an upside-down love. He loves the worthless, the fallen, the broken, the despised and the rejected. They are unburdened by pride and the arrogance that would despise his love, and so he is able to meet them at a point in their lives when they are ready to respond to the gentle stirring of the Holy Spirit who will guide them to the Cross of Christ Jesus, to the incomparable joy of his love, and eternal life.

In the six years since leaving newspapers, God has patiently been teaching me the truth of Proverbs 3:5-6, the hand-written verse reference I found on that scrap of paper on the church floor: 'Trust in the Lord with all your heart and lean not on your own understanding; in all your ways acknowledge him, and he will make your paths straight.'

It has been difficult for me because of the depth of the fears that God has had to work through and break down. He has put me in situations where I could do nothing else but trust in him with all my heart. There have been several such times, and I believed, as he carried me through each one, that I had the strength of faith to trust in him in all circumstances. But I was wrong. The next crisis, worse than the last, would cause me yet again to fall down in my faith.

I do believe this was, and continues to be, all part of God's learning process for me. Each experience took me to a greater test of my faith, and to the edges of a despair which caused me to seem far from God. I would feel such black hopelessness. In the early hours, riven with fear, I would leaf through the pages of my Bible hoping that God would give me some word of encouragement to strengthen me and take me through the day.

Maybe this is not the way that it should be. But it is the way it has been with me. And I did stand, although so feebly. I can say that, to God's glory. I can say that no matter how desperately and fearfully I cried out in my weakness, I continued to praise God and hold on to him.

I have tried to live the words of Paul in the Good News version of Philippians 1:20: 'My deep desire and hope is that I shall never fail in my duty, but that at all times, and especially just now, I shall be full of courage, so that with my whole being I shall bring honour to Christ, whether I live or die.'

Whether I live or die, that is the key. It is the ultimate commitment in serving Christ and it destroys Satan's power in our lives. It removes his grip on our earth-bound fears. If we are prepared to die for Christ, then what physical harm can Satan cause us? The prize he desires—our souls—he can never have. They belong to our God. When I acknowledged that fact it brought into sharper focus what Christ Jesus means to me: that he is my life.

Whether I live or die, frankly, isn't important to me, other than to be with Christ Jesus. But my concerns are for my family, and this is where Satan has succeeded many times in taking me to very edge of the abyss—

through my fears for them and the consequences of my resignation to them. He has used my anxieties for my family to try to separate me from God's power and love. Of course I commit Sue and the children daily to the his protection asking that they will be covered by the blood of Jesus. . . but the fear that I might lose them remains.

God, in permitting Satan's schemes, is presently taking me through these fears, so that I can understand, at another level, to trust in him with all my heart and lean not on my own understanding. I am convinced and reassured by his word that the family is a central to God's creation, which is perhaps why it is under so much threat today, and that what has happened in my life will in time work out to my family's good, so that they may emerge through it all strong and united, and knowing, I pray, Christ Jesus in their lives.

My hope is in the promise of Romans 8:28, 'And we know that in all things God works for the good of those who love him, who have been called according to his purpose.' In God nothing is wasted, everything has a purpose, although it might seem otherwise at the time. Through it all, God is showing us, teaching us, guiding us to understand his will and his ways and to transform us into the image of the Lord Jesus Christ.

No matter how many times we fail, God doesn't give up on us. With him, our failure is never final. No matter how many times we stumble, he will continue to steady us and support us, as our Father reassures us in Psalm 91:14-15: '"Because he loves me," says the Lord, "I will rescue him; I will protect him because he acknowledges my name. He will call upon me, and I will answer him; I will be with him in trouble, I will deliver him and honour him. With long life will I satisfy him and show him my salvation."' And Psalm

24:18: 'The Lord is close to the broken-hearted and saves those who are crushed in spirit." I know the truth of these words.

I remain in great hope for two other reasons. The first is based on what God clearly said to me some months after I left newspapers. It is was through one line in Joel 2:25, which reads: 'I will repay you for the years the locusts have eaten.' I believe, when the time is right, whatever I have lost will be restored, and then my family will see the power and the compassion and the providence of God.

The second cause of my hope is a vision I have had: I see the garden of our home on a mid-summer's day full of children—orphans, the abused, the physically and mentally handicapped—sitting at tables weighed down with ice cream and cakes and all the delights of a garden party. There is a Punch and Judy show and a disco, and dozens of 'Jesus is King' balloons trailing off into the sky. The air is full of the squeals of laughter, and the children are embraced in God's love. Then our house will be a house of joy, and within it will dwell Christ Jesus.

Professionally, matters are in God's hands, as in recent months I have worked to finish this book. Its purpose is to give hope and encouragement to those who, like me, have fallen far short in living out the fullness of the Christian faith.

I have been as candid as I can in my circumstances, so that those who are going through spiritually tough times at the moment might be strengthened by my weaknesses, and it might help them to believe that, no matter what, if our lives are committed to God, his love is with us, and will continue to be with us, through and beyond eternity. In the deep darkness of your times, let that truth burn itself into your heart. And then know the comforting power of God's love and his peace, 'which transcends all understanding' and 'will guard your hearts and minds in Christ Jesus' (Philipians 4:7). I do pray that you will be blessed by that peace in the struggle of your spiritual growth in Christ Jesus.

These years have seen our three eldest children grow into young adults. Sam, his diabetes well under control, is now nineteen and studying law at university. He has become a fine person and a friend. Jessica and Sophie, aged sixteen and seventeen, both incredibly infuriating and beautiful, are mostly studying their hair and eye make-up. Precocious Elizabeth, aged six going on fifteen, is in her second year at infants' school. One of God's blessings has been the joy of her love and friendship.

Toby is twenty-seven, and has had a career change—from chef to computer science student. The thyroid gland complication has been corrected through medication to counter his allergy. I am not sure he knows how proud of him I am. He has done well, despite his father. Alexandra, twenty-nine, has suffered no further epileptic fits, and is halfway through a two-year nursing course. My two grandchildren, Terry, ten, and Jenny, eight, are mischievously healthy. Alexandra, too, has done well. She is a brave girl whose fighting spirit has overcome many disadvantages. I have lost contact with step-daughter, Janice, and her mother, Gwen, but my prayers are with them daily.

The Wild Bunch have now left town at last, and Sue, having successfully passed a word processor/secretarial course, is doing well as an office administrator. She has shown tremendous courage and fortitude in the most difficult times. I know there have been many occasions when my commitment to Christ has been hard for her to understand or accept.

My constant prayer is that one day she, and the rest of my family, will come to know the love of Christ Jesus. Then they will understand why there could be no other road.

I have chosen you and have not rejected you.
So do not fear, for I am with you;
do not be dismayed, for I am your God.
I will strengthen you and help you;
I will uphold you with my righteous right hand
(Isaiah 41:9-10)

Let the peace of Christ rule in your hearts. . .
(Colossians 3:15)